praise for masala

"The Masala Mamas' Kitchen reflects the strength and voice th[at has been] found thanks to GPM's initiatives. The stories and recipes will n[…]"

  -Mandie Winston, Executive Director, JDC Global Response, Innovative Development (GRID)

"Many themes run through the Masala Mamas Cookbook. One most important factor is about the powerful role of a woman in society and dedication towards their responsibilities. The book is not only a combination of various Indian recipes but also gives a homely feeling. All the ingredients used are natural and authentic. The recipes are nutritionally balanced. In short it is a bunch of beautifully crafted recipes that gives an insight into the Indian home kitchen. It is a remarkable book not only written skillfully but with a rare mix of loving attention and a deep sense of culinary art of an Indian woman."

  -Chef Prashant Tikadia, Executive Chef - Meluha The Fern & Rodas, an Ecotel Hotel

"It's 8 am. Shivaji Nagar, a neighbourhood 10 minutes away from Kalwa East railway station is stirring awake to the sound of devotional music playing on a loudspeaker. Among a row of shuttered shops, a 10x15 feet kitchen witnesses a flurry of activity. Five women, wearing polka dot aprons and scrub caps, are preparing 25 kilos of dal khichdi. The simple, hearty dish will feed 100 underprivileged children who study in class 1 to 4 of Joshua Greenberger Learning Centre, a school run by non-profit Gabriel Project Mumbai (GPM)."

  -Krutika Behrawala, Mid-day newspaper

"We can all learn from the way [the Masala Mamas] share their love and dedication with their children, families and community, through cooking."

  -Dr. Darren Weiss, President, Humble Smile Foundation

"Nothing is more precious to parents than good nutrition for their growing children, and the chance for improving their children's life chances provided by education…Gabriel Project Mumbai (GPM) brings these two strong motivations together in a simple but beautiful way…Together we can change the world, one child at a time."

  - Huseyin Arslan and Andrew Jacobs
  Chairman, AGT Foods & Ingredients and Director, AGT Poortman, respectively

"We could not be prouder of the Masala Mamas."

  -Naomi Eisenberger, Executive Director, Co-Founder, Good People Fund

"The Masala Mamas cookbook is about so much more than food. It is about women's lives, cultures, and friendships. This cookbook is a must-have for anyone interested in empowering women around the world."

  -Erin Zaikis, Founder, Sundara

"We are so proud of Gabriel Project Mumbai and Masala Mamas and believe that the cookbook amplifies their work!"

  -Dyonna Ginsburg, Executive Director, OLAM

"The Masala Mamas cookbook is a wonderful initiative from Gabriel Project Mumbai…empower[ing] people, in particular women and children, to break free from poverty."

  -Dr Judith Stanton, Chief Executive, Tzedek

Proceeds from this book go to the Masala Mamas,
a non-profit social enterprise promoting
nutrition, literacy, health,
women's empowerment, and community development
in the Kalwa slum in Thane, India.

Gabriel Project Mumbai

www.gabrielprojectmumbai.org
www.masalamamas.org
info@gabrielprojectmumbai.org

Masala Mamas:
Recipes and stories from Indian women changing their communities through food and love

Elana Sztokman, PhD
Editor
With Hayley Dsouza

Indu Sona Mane
Sangita Raut
Alka Harishchandra Gaikwad
Hirabai Vilas Umbarkar
Jayshree Chavdry
Jayshree Kondwal
Kalpana Gawde
Kamal Shivaji Kadam
Mangal Vittal Mane
Manisha Sable
Maya Kadu
Ragini Godbole
Ranjana Ramchandra Gaikwad
Rohini Mahamuni
Subhadra Khose
Usha Pipre

www.masalamamas.org

Lioness
An imprint of Panoma Press

Masala Mamas: Recipes and Stories from Indian Women Changing their Communities through Food and Love

First published in 2018 by

Panoma Press
48 St Vincent Drive, St Albans, Herts, AL1 5SJ, UK

info@panomapress.com
www.panomapress.com

Book layout by Shoshana Balofsky

Printed on acid-free paper from managed forests.

ISBN 9781784529000

The right of Elana Sztokman to be identified as the author of this work has been asserted in accordance with sections 77 and 78 of the Copyright, Designs and Patents Act 1988.

A CIP catalogue record for this book is available from the British Library.

All rights reserved. No part of this book may be reproduced in any material form (including photocopying or storing in any medium by electronic means and whether or not transiently or incidentally to some other use of this publication) without the written permission of the copyright holder except in accordance with the provisions of the Copyright, Designs and Patents Act 1988. Applications for the Copyright holder's written permission to reproduce any part of this publication should be addressed to the publishers.
This book is available online and in bookstores.
Copyright 2018 Elana Sztokman

Printed in India by Imprint Press

contents

Preface by Huseyin Arslan and Andrew Jacobs ... ix
Preface by Audrey Axelrod Trachtma ... x

Introductions — 1-32
Meet the Masala Mamas ... 2
Enter the Maharashtrian Kitchen ... 7
A Visual Guide of Spices, Lentils, and Leaves ... 11
Kitchen Essentials ... 12
Substitutions ... 20
Conversions and Measurements ... 21
Key to Symbols ... 25
Glossary ... 26
Map of Women's Villages in Maharashtra ... 32

Recipes and Stories

SECTION 1: Getting Started — 33-48
Recipe List ... 33
The Pujah ... 34

SECTION 2: Drinks — 49-62
Recipe List ... 49
Spices of Life ... 50
Meet Indu Mane ... 54
Meet Manisha Sable ... 60

SECTION 3: Breads — 63-76
Recipe List ... 63
Fasting Foods ... 64
A Boatride to Alibag ... 70

SECTION 4: Breakfast Foods — 77-92
Recipe List ... 77
Festival Foods ... 78
Meet Sangita Raut ... 84

SECTION 5: Dips — 93-114
Recipe List ... 93
Cosmetic foods ... 94
Meet Alka Gaikwad ... 100

Meet Maya Kadu	104
Meet Hayley Dsouza	112

SECTION 6: Snacks and Finger Foods — 115-142
Recipe List	115
The Evolution of Arranged Marriages	116
Meet Kamal Shivaji Kadam	124
Soup and Study	134
Meet Subhadra Khose	140

SECTION 7: Mains — 143-180
Recipe List	143
The Status of Women in India	144
Healing Malnutrition in Babies	150
Meet Kalpana Gawde	166
Meet Ragini Goldbole	174

SECTION 8: Sweets — 181-202
Recipe List	181
Yield: 100	182
Meet Hirabai Umbarkar	190
Meet Mangal Vittal Mane	198

Extras — 203-218
Index of the Women's Recipes	204
About Gabriel Project Mumbai	205
Our NGO Partners	207
Our Sponsors	208
Index	209
About the Authors	215
Acknowledgments	216
Credits	216

"Tilgul ghyaa, goad-goad bola"

तीळ गुळ घ्या गोड गोड बोला

"Accept this sweet and utter sweet words"

A customary Maharashtrian exchange on the festival of Makar Sankranti

◇◇◇◇◇◇◇◇◇◇◇◇◇

This book is dedicated to:

The people of AGT Foods & Ingredients, India,
and to our friend Andrew Jacobs
who made this book possible.

To our friend, Sarah Gribetz.

And most importantly, to the children of the
GPM Love2Learn school in Kalwa, India,
who are eating food made from the stuff of love and dreams.

From Producer to the World

FILIX - 401 D Fourth Floor
L.B.S. Marg, Bhandup (West)
Mumbai INDIA 400 078

Ph: 022-61470 470
www.agtfoods.com
www.alliancegrain.in

Nothing is more precious to parents than good nutrition for their growing children, and the chance for improving their children's life chances provided by education.

Gabriel Project Mumbai (GPM) brings these two strong motivations together in a simple but beautiful way. If the parents send their children to GPM's school (instead of to work or scavenging) then GPM will feed them a hot, nutritious lunch. Well-nourished children learn quicker and better than hungry children.

AGT Foods & Ingredients Inc. is a global food company, headquartered in Canada, with operations and activity in all major agricultural regions. Although a large public company, our roots are in family-owned entrepreneurial activities and we operate as one large global family.

Our main activity is in sourcing and shipping Pulses - peas, beans, lentils & chickpeas - so we are delighted to partner with GPM in the publication of this cookbook, sharing wonderful recipes, many featuring Pulses, from the Masala Mamas who cook for GPM's students.

Pulses are increasingly recognised for their strong contribution to health, nutrition, sustainability and affordability. The United Nations designated 2016 as "International Year of Pulses" to recognise their contribution to global food security and health.

We are happy to sponsor the production costs of this beautiful cookbook, so every cent you spend on acquiring your copy will go directly to helping feed and educate more children in Mumbai's slums. Together we can change the world, one child at a time.

Please give generously and buy extra copies of this cookbook as gifts for your friends and family.

Huseyin Arslan
Chairman, AGT Foods & Ingredients
President, Global Pulse Confederation

Andrew Jacobs
Director, AGT Poortman
UK Friends of Gabriel Project Mumbai

It gives me great pleasure to be part of this project. This cookbook tells the story of 16 women in the Kalwa slum of Mumbai who come together every day — 6 days a week, 11 months a year — to prepare, cook, and deliver hundreds of lunches for the students who attend the Gabriel Project Mumbai (GPM) Love2Learn school in the Kalwa slum. These women are proud, strong, capable and friendly. And they are making a difference in the lives of children. But they are making a difference in their own lives, too.

I visited Mumbai in February 2017 where I encountered the work of GPM, an organization that was started in 2012 to care for vulnerable children in the Mumbai slums, to prevent child labor, disease, hunger and illiteracy and enable children to go to school. During that visit, I had the opportunity to meet the women whose recipes and stories are in this cookbook. I profoundly enjoyed talking with them and learning about their lives.

In some ways, they are very traditional. They belong to the Marathi Hindu community, and were wed in arranged marriages in their villages before the age of eighteen. In other ways, they are pioneers. For many, this is their first job outside the home, and their husbands are supportive of the change, encouraging their newfound independence.

Sangita, for example, one of the leaders of the group, has been married for 22 years and has four children – three girls and one boy. She was 15 when she got married and first saw her husband only at the wedding. She notes that as long as her children married within the Marathi culture, she would not be opposed to them choosing a "love marriage" (as opposed to an arranged marriage).

The women in the group all share one thing in common: they all moved from their villages — where they had clean air, land, extended family, communal traditions and histories — to give their children a better education and a better life. In their villages, many schools close down or stop after fifth grade due to the outflow of people; higher levels of grade schools are too far away to be practical options. In searching for something better for their children in the urban slum of Mumbai, they make sure that their children learn English, math, Marathi and Hindi.

Today, the Kalwa slum is home. Most of the women have been in Kalwa for 15 years or more, and an estimated 80-90% of the families own their homes. Still, there is little garbage collection in the slums. So while their homes and the paths in front of them are neat and clean, the garbage thrown directly into the river behind their homes breeds disease in the monsoon season when the river overflows its banks into the neighborhoods. Sometimes they receive water for only a few hours a day so water is stored in their homes in large containers for when they need it, and there are no modern conveniences such as washing machines or dryers. Everything is labor intensive and requires significant amounts of time.

The cooperative that they built through the work of GPM has become something much larger and significant than economic development. These women have created a community together, a social framework to fill in what they lost after leaving their villages. This cookbook tells the story of creating connection to the past while building a vision for a better future.

Audrey Axelrod Trachtman
GPM board member, January 2018

www.gabrielprojectmumbai.org | info@gabrielprojectmumbai.org
Gabriel Project Mumbai is a registered not-for-profit 501(c)3, EIN 45-4541556

meet the masala mamas?

By Elana Sztokman

Indu Sona Mane is a busy woman. She wakes up every day at 4:30am to do the washing and cleaning of her one-and-a-half room home in the Kalwa slum in the Thane district in northern Mumbai. Then Indu starts cooking her husband's lunch and preparing snacks for her children. Afterwards she has a bath and cares for herself. Only then does she set out to work, trekking through the alleys of Kalwa, arriving at the Delicio Women's Cooperative kitchen by 7:30am. That's when her other work begins.

Indu, the 38-year-old mother of two originally from the village of Sangli, Maharashtra, is a manager of the Delicio kitchen where 16 women of Kalwa produce and deliver meals every day for hundreds of children in school.

This is not as simple as it sounds. She and her team of 16 women work out of a space of 12 square meters – smaller than an average American child's bedroom – which has industrial kitchen utensils but does not always have electricity or running water. Still, the food is always fresh and flavorful, and always cheap. The cost of a hot meal for one child in the slums is roughly 35 cents. When they eat well, everyone is happy. Especially Indu.

The women are part of a program started in 2012 by an NGO called Gabriel Project Mumbai aimed at promoting education, healthcare, and nutrition for children living in the slums. An abundance of research points to the invaluable impact of education in halting cycles of poverty. Unfortunately, when poverty is so acute that families are unsure whether they will have food the next day, the long-term goal of education is often deferred in order to stave off the immediate crisis of hunger. Children in difficult urban slums, even as young as five years old, sometimes work in terrible conditions as sewage cleaners and rag-pickers just to earn a few rupees for food.

The women offer a powerful solution to this harrowing problem of child labor: food in school. Laboring every day in a kitchen supported by the aptly named "Good People Fund", the women create abundant incentives for kids to stay in school. After all, when parents in Kalwa find out that the school provides hot meals, they are eager to send their kids to learn. It's a win-win. Children eat. And they learn. Parents are relieved. Short-term hunger is resolved. Long-term education is on the way. And the women work. They are building a food-service social enterprise that gives them and their families economic empowerment and nutrition for the children. In this model, everyone benefits.

Interestingly, former US President Bill Clinton said the same thing. At a speech at Yale University in October 2013, he offered a passionate plea for providing food to children who go to school, using food as an incentive to advance education. "A billion people in this world cannot read a single word in any language, not one. 120 million children never go to school," he said, adding that "every year of schooling adds 10 to 15 percent a year to the incomes of people in poor countries for life." The solution, he said, was simple: give parents incentives to send their kids to school. The most profound incentive? Food. "This is not rocket science," he said, and it is not "just idle talk. This stuff works."[2]

Indeed, this is exactly what Gabriel Project Mumbai and the women of the Delicio cooperative – the "Masala Mamas" – are accomplishing with the children in Kalwa. After the program's first year, teachers reported a 50 percent increase in attendance. Though the long-term impact is yet to be felt, one can begin to extrapolate the impact for these children.

Today, GPM operates its own school, the Love2Learn school, with branches in Kalwa as well as in remote rural villages in the Palgar district of Maharashtra. The vision of Love2Learn takes a holistic view of children's needs and community development. This means not only sustaining a multi-faceted, creative, student-centered learning environment, but also providing regular on-site heathcare, as well as free, hot, nutritious meals to the students every day. It is the GPM "Triad of Children's Wellbeing": attending to education, health and nutrition all at once.

This approach has implications for the entire community. These daily meals are provided by women of the community, who are supporting in build their social enterprise while they in turn ensure that the children's basic needs are met.

---

2 William J. Clinton . Transcript of 'Global Challenges', A public address given by former US President William J. Clinton at Yale University on October 31, 2003. Friday, October 31, 2003 http://yaleglobal.yale.edu/content/transcript-global-challenges

The Masala Mamas are a devoted and passionate group. When they arrive each morning at the Delicio kitchen, they first perform rituals to fill their space with dedication, respect, and love. They start their day by making a special powder dye for tikkas or bindis – dots of dye that they place on one another's foreheads while giving each other blessings for health, prosperity, success, joy, or whatever they need at that moment. One woman needs a special blessing for her ailing husband. Another's child has a big exam in school. This is where they receive emotional and spiritual support to get through their days. They smile at each other, close their eyes, and wish each other well with sincerity and depth. These are not rote rituals but honest and profound exchanges of goodwill. They do these "Puja" rituals, lighting incense, praying to different gods – Durga or Ganesh to remove obstacles; Lakshmi for abundance – to direct their minds and their actions. They fill the kitchen with spiritual energies of gratitude, humility, and most of all love, energies that filter through into everything that they do. They are not just providing food for the children in the community. They are also filling the neighborhood, and their own circle, with love.

I have a special connection to the program: the founder of GPM, Jacob Sztokman, is my spouse of 26 years. He started this program in 2012 after visiting India and being touched by the children in Kalwa. He was working in marketing at a hi-tech company at the time, and a woman on his team from Mumbai introduced him to her father, who is involved in an NGO called REAP that delivers education to children in Kalwa. Her father arranged for Jacob to visit Kalwa and see the work that REAP and other NGOs are doing on behalf of the community. He was deeply moved. Irreversibly altered. His life would never be the same.

For months after that visit, Jacob could not stop thinking about the children he met – children, he says, who in some cases were the same age as our own children, who could have been anyone's children. He spent months sitting up at night learning more, talking to the people in Kalwa, trying to figure out a way to get involved. Finally, the people at REAP told him something very simple and powerful. They were running classes, they said, but often had trouble convincing families to send their children to learn – all because of the lack of food. The reason why little children, even as young as five years old, are often sent to work in terrible jobs is because of food. The few rupees that children may acquire may make the difference between whether the child eats or doesn't eat that day.

The solution was simple: provide hot meals in schools, they said. And so that's what Jacob decided to do. He left his job and started a program for hot meals in schools.

And who did he approach to make those meals? The women of the community.

Indu has been managing this operation for five years now with mastery, skill and attention to detail – even though she never completed fifth grade. She wanted to stay in school, she told me as we sat on the floor of the kitchen eating egg pulav, potato bhaji, ghavan, and gajar halwa that the women made. Her teachers knew she was smart, she said. Even her parents knew she was special. But like so many other Indian families, they had other plans for their daughter. She had to look after her younger brother and help out with the household. And, of course, she had to prepare for marriage. These things took priority. Her teacher trekked to her parents' house and begged them to let her stay in school. The teacher even offered to let Indu sleep at her house. But the family declined. Indu is still angry about it.

I could feel Indu's pain. Women and girls all around the world have been sacrificing their own aspirations and educations for the sake of their brothers' educations, or for the sake of family needs, for hundreds of years, maybe thousands. It was only a few generations ago that this practice began to be challenged in Europe and the United States. As I listen to Indu, I am aware of my intense luck and privilege of having received a full-blown education, and of how close our stories are - my great-grandmothers faced similar expectations to marry at the age of 12 or 13 and to give up their education on behalf of everyone else. Indu and I certainly come from different worlds – we live in different countries, speak different languages, and worship different religions. I am a Jewish, English-speaking, woman originally from New York and now Israel; Indu is a Marathi-speaking, Hindu woman living in Kalwa, Maharashtra, India. And yet, despite those gaps, from a historical perspective, we share the experience as navigating this world as women – a world in which gender cultures are evolving, some faster than others, but still impact the course of our lives. I carry the stories of my grandmothers and great-grandmothers wherever I go, even as I navigate the paths of the Kalwa slum with Indu and the rest of the women.

Indu is not alone. Each of the women has a similar story. They all left remote villages years ago in search of a better life and landed here in the Kalwa slum. They all got what they were in search of – education for their children and a chance at a stronger economic future. But for all of them, the transition came with some steep prices: loss of fresh air, loss of community, loss of connection to the land, and loss of extended families and traditions that were once right at their doorstep. For the women, the meaning of the work in the kitchen collective is not only about feeding the children but also about making a better future for themselves. Some of the women had never worked outside the house before, some do not know how to read and write, and some do not even have enough math education to figure out the age difference between themselves and their children.

That is the world they came from. But their children are different. The children are educated – some of them work as bankers, pharmacists, or computer engineers. Many of their daughters are working and studying, some in the sciences. This is a remarkable story of change and mobility. Within one or two generations, the women have the ability to transform their families from living in remote rural poverty to living western, educated middle-class lives. It is a change that is taking place because of the power and strength of these women. Driven by giving their children opportunities that they did not have, the women are the catalysts for momentous social change. We know that when women thrive, entire communities benefit. These are the women who are creating a gentle but potent revolution in India, modeling change and opportunity. With these new outlets and opportunities, the Masala Mamas are providing for their children and also for themselves in new ways.

introduction

The women shared their stories with me for this book. They told me about their histories, their migrations from villages, their dreams for their children's future, and sometimes even their visions for themselves. I am honored to be able to record those stories and share them here. I hope I do the women justice. My goal is for the book to be a tool for strengthening the women's voices and bringing their cultural knowledge and their work in this world.

This is not your ordinary cookbook, because it is not just about cooking. This is a story about women who use their deep love of cooking as an instrument for social change. It is about women who bring their spiritual heritage around food into everything that they do, promoting a culture and lifestyle of friendship, connection, and care as they work to make a real difference in the lives of some of the most vulnerable children in the world. They know what they are trying to do: keep the children in school. And they know that providing food with love in school gives kids the best chance at changing the trajectory of their lives.

A note about me: I am wearing two "hats" in compiling this cookbook – and neither one of them involves cooking. Professionally, I am a writer, researcher and anthropologist specializing in women's lives, and especially women in traditional societies. Personally, I am married to the founder of Gabriel Project Mumbai (GPM), as I mentioned, the NGO that created this project. Of all the amazing projects that GPM is working on, this is the one that touched my heart the most. I decided that I wanted to write about the women, and explore the ways in which their work is having powerful ripple effects, transforming the community and their own lives.

The book is divided into sections by food course – breads, dips, drinks, savory snacks, mains, sweet snacks and desserts. But scattered throughout each of these sections are profiles of the women, as well as essays exploring aspects of Maharashtrian women's culture.

Enjoy this book – the tastes, the colors, the aromas, the stories, and the spirit. Ingest the love that the women have put into their work. And share these stories with the people in your life, too. You are now part of this story, of women changing the world through food, friendship and love.

enter the maharashtrian kitchen

The women squat on the floor of the kitchen, their colorful saris blanketing their bodies with only their ring-decorated feet showing. They lean over bowls and boards, sifting through lentils and rice, kneading dough, and grinding spices. Their bracelets clank through the chatter, noises of food and friendship, Kalwa-style.

This is how the women cook.

It all starts on the floor, with a lot of preparation and attention to details that are second nature to them. Ingredients are fresh, colorful, and aromatic. There are no canned goods, no frozen vegetables or greens, and no shortcuts. Every dish requires steps of preparation – the grinding, the soaking, the pre-roasting. Some recipes take multiple days or more. The longest recipe in this book, the mango pickle, takes two weeks of watching chopped raw mango sitting in the sun. Hayley Dsouza, whose mother is the source of this particular dish, recalls how when she was a child, she and her brother were tasked with "guarding" the mango as it pickled, sneaking occasional pieces along the way.

There is also no oven. Although different areas of India do have food cultures that include ovens – like the famous Tandoori oven in the north – here in Kalwa, cooking is stovetop only. Even cakes and breads are prepared in a pan. The only oven-based recipe included in this cookbook is the pav bread, a type of wheat-based, western-style dinner roll that is very popular in Mumbai. Everything else, including desserts, is made on the stovetop.

The women know what they have to do, with the planning stages etched in their minds like a thumbprint on a balushahi. Everyday spice mixtures like Garam Masala or the famous Maharashtrian Goda Masala are prepared in advance in bulk, ready to be used in almost every kind of dish. The making of ghee, the Indian clarified butter that forms the foundation of many dishes – used for everything from heating mustard seeds to spreading on naan – takes skill and practice

to master well. It is an amazing food with many medicinal properties, and can survive outside of the refrigerator for months at a time, as long as it doesn't touch water. The women hold this knowledge tight. They know which kind of flour goes with which cooking method, the different life stages of mangoes and tomatoes, the various lengths that different lentils need to soak – anywhere from an hour to a day. Their hands, noses and eyes hold an encyclopedic archive of their ancestral food practices.

The women cook using all that knowledge in a precise, attentive way. There is almost no such thing as throwing a few things into a pot. There is an order, a process, a build-up of flavor. The cooking requires thought, devotion, and heart. And lots of spices.

The truth is, though, there really is no such thing as "Indian cooking". There are many, many Indian styles of cooking. The varieties in foods are as diverse as the people of India. This should hardly come as a surprise. India, the largest democracy in the world, with a population of over 1.2 billion people – including hundreds of tribes, 12 major languages, a space that covers one of the widest ranges of ecosystems in the world (massive areas of dense forests alongside inhabitable dry desert and some 7500 kilometers of coastlines) – a country this vast can hardly be imagined to have uniform culinary styles.

Food practices are influenced by geography, climate, altitude, social class, religion, history, and tradition, all of which are sources of great diversity across India. What you have is what you eat. Women, who have been responsible for most of the world's cooking for millennia, are experts at using resources that are readily available to them in their cooking. Cooking styles reflect realities such as which fruits and vegetables are native to an area, whether a region is landlocked or coastal, whether the land is fertile all year round or whether preservation methods are vital, and combinations of spices based on recipes passed down from generation to generation in families, tribes and villages.

Moreover, there are vast differences between wheat-based agricultural areas and rice-based farming. While we tend to think of Indian food as incorporating both rice dishes and chapatti dishes, wheat and rice reflect two very different agricultural processes with different culinary results. In fact, *The New York Times* even argued that rice-culture versus wheat-culture has a deep impact on personality, political views, attitude towards life, decision-making, and cognitive functioning.[2] The women in the collective, for example, are aware of who in the group comes from wheat-growing villages and who comes from rice-growing villages.

All of this affects the variations in Indian cooking. Thus, while much of India eats in the style of "thali meals" – that is, meals served on a kind of one-course dinner plate filled with colorful and aromatic bowls of chutneys, pickles, dals, flatbreads and sweets – the actual foods that are placed on the thali differ from state to state. The thalis in the north-western state of Rajasthan, the largest and most popular tourist state with its abundance of palaces and forts ("raja" means

---

[2] TM Luhrmann, Wheat People vs. Rice People: Why Are Some Cultures More Individualistic Than Others? *New York Times*, Dec. 3, 2014 https://www.nytimes.com/2014/12/04/opinion/why-are-some-cultures-more-individualistic-than-others.html

"regal"), are influenced by its grand, regal culture as well as the fact that it is mostly desert. Their dishes tend to be rich, colorful and grandiose, like their famous Dal Bati delicacy of lentil stew and special charcoal-baked bread and they use few fresh vegetables, relying instead on preserved and pickled dishes. They also use dried fruits and nuts in abundance, which are considered a luxury. Three-quarters of the population are vegetarian, although the non-vegetarian population, a group called "Rajputs", have their culinary impact too.

The thalis in the western state of Gujarat, by contrast, a state of 62 million people that is loaded with lush hills, fertile plains, and water-drenched expanses, are full of fresh vegetables and grains. Gujarat cooks are known for experimentation and variety, and foodies trek to Gujarat from all over India to try new cuisine. In addition to rice and vegetables, Gujarat is also famous for dishes based on millet, sugarcane, peanuts, and sesame. These dishes use a lot of dairy and Gujarat cuisine is also primarily vegetarian. Gujarat is famous for foods such as the millet-based bread called dhebra, and the spongy, untranslatable dish called dhokla which is made of a fermented batter containing rice and split-peas.

Maharashtra, a state in western India with a population of 114 million people, also has its own distinct styles. Mumbai, the largest city in the state of Maharashtra, which is where this book is centered, is famous for street foods like pav bhaji, bhel puri, and pani puri. The lush and tropical Konkan Coast is the source for coconuts, mangoes, Indian berries, kokum fruit, and jaggery (sugarcane extract), that feature prominently in the Maharashtrian menu. A wide array of fish and seafood are also very popular in this region with its long coastline and the fact that Mumbai is surrounded on three sides by water. In Mumbai, freshly-squeezed sugarcane juice is available on street corners everywhere for a few rupees, as is coconut juice that you drink by sticking a straw into a coconut. These are not the brown fuzzy coconuts that are popular in Hawaiian imagery, but rather lime green, soft-skinned coconuts native to this region. Both street-drinks are not only refreshing in Mumbai heat but also full of medicinal properties and health benefits. Sugarcane juice, for example, is credited with a range of properties from cancer prevention and digestive healing, to clearing up skin and aiding in weight loss. In fact, many native Maharashtrian fruits and vegetables are used heartily in Ayurveda Indian medicine, such as the kokum fruit – which is included in recipes here – or the moringa plant, among many others.

While geography and climate are arguably the most prominent influencers of cuisine in India, religious traditions also play a key role in culinary identity. There are many dishes that are associated with religious rituals and festivals. For instance, there is a vast tradition throughout India of "fasting foods" or "upwas", foods you eat when you are fasting. A "fast" or "vrat" in Hinduism does not mean banning all eating and drinking. Although traditions vary, it usually means avoiding – often for only part of a day – heavy grains like wheat and rice, as well as lentils, onions, garlic, salt, and meat. However lighter grains like buckwheat, tapioca, or millet as well as dairy, fruits and vegetables are allowed. These practices, which vary in frequency and intensity, have generated a wide range of special upwas, some of which are included in the cookbook. Indians can go into eateries all around the country and request a fasting menu. And typically, when the women of the collective fast, they carry upwas around with them so they are never too hungry.

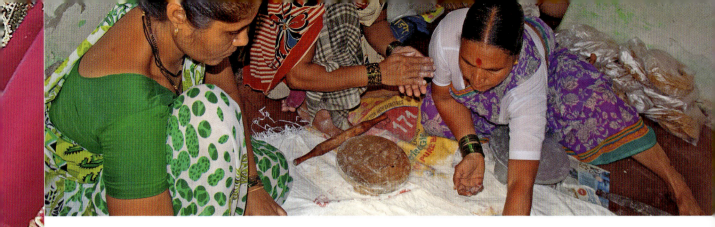

India is also known for its many colorful festivals during the year, which vary in the way they are celebrated in different states. Maharashtrian festival traditions often incorporate their own unique rituals and foods. Sangita Raut, one of the women in the collective, describes how Nag Panchami, a festival that celebrates the snake god, requires a food called Kanevle made out of a batter of dal (lentils) and jaggery that is cooked, boiled and then "fed" to the snake god along with milk.

For the popular Makar Sankranti festival that marks the sun's journey into the northern hemisphere, observed on January 14 every year, the women make a dish called Ambil that they offer in the Ram temple. Every family has to make this once a year. It is made of jowar (sorghum flour) and turmeric, and has to be soaked in water for two days before the cooking begins. This festival is also known for a unique Maharashtrian tradition of exchanging Til-Gul Ladoo, special sweets made from sesame seeds and jaggery, as tokens of goodwill while greeting each other with the words "*til-gul ghyaa, aani goad-goad bolaa*" meaning "Accept this til-gul (sweet) and utter sweet words". The gesture is meant to enter the year with feelings of goodwill while letting go of arguments and disagreements.

Indu also recalls making Faral, a collection of special sweets prepared for the festival of Diwali. When she was a child she learned how to make Faral – her aunts, sisters-in-law, cousins, neighbors used to come together and prepare it. But now Indu has to make it all alone. Still, she always thinks about how much fun it was to make these sweets with all the women together and longs for those days.

As much as the women make food, the food makes the women. These cultures around food create a particular kind of women's experience, which at times involves communal labor and service as well as a coming-together to a space of sharing and togetherness. When the women move from villages to the city, much of that culture is permanently on pause in a way that they describe as a loss for themselves. The women's collective has thus enabled women to re-gather and form communities in new and different ways yet still around women's cultures of food, in order to fill the void of the separation of their families and loved ones so far away.

This coming together in the Kalwa kitchen represents change – working outside of the home, building economic stability, and promoting a strong education for the children. But it also represents tradition: women nurturing each other, sharing the time-consuming tasks of aspects of Indian cooking, and preserving the practices and customs of food that are important to them. Together, they are connected to their narratives, their traditions, and their memories while they work towards social change. They are sitting on a crossroads between past and present, using their histories to nourish the next generation. Their stories merge, too, as they learn from each other, support each other, and build a new future.

a visual guide to spices, leaves and lentils

introductions

spices

Ajwain
(Carom Seeds)

Amchur
(Mango Powder)

Asafoetida
(Hing)

Bay Leaves

Cardamom Pods, Black

Cardamom Pods, Green

Cardamom, Ground

Cinnamon Sticks

Cloves, Whole

Coconut, Ground

Coriander Seeds

Coriander, Ground

Cumin Seeds
(Jeera)

Cumin, Ground

Fennel Seeds

Fenugreek Seeds

introduction

Ginger	Jaggery (Sugarcane)	Mustard Seeds, Black	Mustard Seeds, Yellow

Peppercorns	Red Chili, Dried and Ground	Red Chilis, Dried	Sesame Seeds, Black

Sesame Seeds, White	Star Anise, Whole	Tamarind	Turmeric

introductions

lentils

Black Eyed Peas (Chowli or Lubia)

Black Gram Lentils (Urad Dal)

Brown Lentils

Chickpeas (Safud Chana)

Mung Beans

Red Lentils (Masoor Dal)

Split Peas

Split Pigeon Peas (Toor Dal)

Yellow Split Peas (Moong Dal)

leaves

Coriander

Curry

Dill

Fenugreek Leaves (Methi)

Mint

Parsley

tips, tricks, conversions and substitutions

Kitchen Essentials

The recipes in this book call for many kitchen tools, some of which are standard in kitchens around the world: a big pot, a frying pan, a sharp knife, cutting board, peeler, measuring tools, colander (or sieve), and plates for serving. Those same items are needed here. But there are also a few other tools that Maharashtrians have in their kitchens that would be helpful to have for many of the recipes in this book (although substitutions that you find in your kitchen can often be used).

Kadai/ Karahi/ Kadhai

A heavy, deep and wide oval pot that is the standard go-to pot in most recipes, sometimes referred to as "the Indian wok".

Tawa/ Tava

A flat griddle, used to fry chapattis and many other flat breads and pancakes.

Pressure Cooker

Used to cut down on cooking times in many recipes, especially those with rice, lentils and pulses. The favorite Indian versions uses "whistles" to measure time, and several recipes call on cooking times based on how many "whistles" there are. In this cookbook, we have tried to estimate the time as best as we can.

Chaki Belan

A board and small rolling pin, much lighter and quicker than a standard American heavy rolling pin, essential for kneading dough.

Coffee Grinder, Mortar and Pestle, or Shil Noda

Any one of these tools for grinding spices. Each of these does the trick, but best to find your favorite tool and technique.

Jhaara

A slotted spoon that is used for removing dumplings from the oil after deep frying. It is helpful to have a small one and a large one, for different sized dumplings and fritters.

Big and Little Net Strainer

For making paneer and other processes as well.

Cheese Cloth

For straining both paneer and ghee.

Steaming Pot or Bamboo Steamer

For steaming vegetables as well as some dough-based snacks.

Idli Rack

Steamer set for preparing "idlis", spongy little pancakes that are eaten with dips.

Appam Patra

A cross between a frying pan and cupcake tin, used for making special dumplings called "appes".

Canning Equipment

Some chutneys, pastes, masalas and dips are best stored in sealed jars. Learning about "canning" techniques can be very useful, but requires canning jars, canning lids, and/or pressure canners. There are canning kits available that have all the parts you need for this process.

Flours

A typical western kitchen usually has one or two types of flour at the most – wheat and perhaps whole wheat flours. Where there are gluten sensitivities, some people will use alternatives such as soy flour. In an Indian kitchen, on the other hand, there may be up to ten different types of flour. Indian cooks know the subtle differences between these flours. The most common flour is actually besan, also called gram flour, which is made of chickpeas and is considered the best binder. This is especially useful in a cooking culture that rarely uses eggs. Rice flour is also popular and is used for many pancake-type recipes such as dosas. There are also lighter flours and some lesser known varieties that are especially popular on "fast" days, during which people are forbidden from consuming "heavy" flours like wheat, rice, or gram flour. These include tapioca, millet, sorghum, and amaranth flour, each of which has its own unique texture and flavor.

Here is a brief guide to the flours included in this cookbook:

Atta	whole grain wheat flour
Besan	chickpea-based gram flour, gluten-free, and considered the best binding flour used for batters, fritters, and pancakes
Chawal ka atta	rice flour, gluten-free, used for breads and pancakes like rotis and dosas
Jowar	sorghum, a very special gluten-free flour, full of health benefits; considered a "superfood"
Maida	an all-purpose white (wheat) flour
Ragi flour	millet flour, gluten-free, used for rotis, upma and other recipes
Rajgira ka atta	amaranth flour, gluten free, high-protein, and a good replacement for flour known as a "fasting" flour for the Hindu fasts; considered a "superfood"
Sabudana flour	tapioca flour, gluten-free, used as a strong binding base that absorbs other flavors; also used as a "fasting" flour
Sooji	semolina, often used as a thickening agent
Soy flour	gluten-free, high in protein, and goes well mixed with other flours

Is it possible to use wheat flour in place of the flours listed in the recipes? The answer is a bit complicated. You can certainly try and experiment as such, knowing that this is going to alter the taste and texture of the food you are making. Each recipe calls for a specific flour as each one has different cooking properties. The rice flour pancake (dosa), for example feels and tastes different from the besan pancake (dhirdi), and from the wheat flour pancake (puri). All three pancakes are delicious and versatile, but they are actually quite different from each other.

As much as possible, try to stick to the flour that the recipe calls for. Most of the recipes are good for people with gluten intolerance, candida issues, and other gastro ailments by using, for example, besan (chickpea flour) or jowar (sorghum flour). Finding recipes to suit those needs should be quite doable.

That said, I would also highly encourage cooks to experiment using some of these flours as replacements for wheat flour. Getting to know these grains has many benefits for the palate as well as the digestive system, and experimenting with these will help you decide for yourself which replacements will work. For instance, tapioca flour is very popular for the fasters, but it has its own unique texture and can change the way you have to handle batter. Gram flour can be great if you are trying not to use eggs, but it can also be a little dry if overused, so you need the right balance. Experimentation will help you get to know your flours, and that is worth the effort. It will help you expand your culinary repertoire and create your own doughy textures and flavors.

Oils

Most of the recipes in this cookbook call for oil or ghee. Ghee is clarified butter and is the go-to oil for most of these recipes. It is cheap and easy to make, and keeps for a long time unrefrigerated.

However, most recipes that call for ghee can also use other oils as replacements. For most recipes, the best kind of oil is a "neutral" oil, such as sunflour, soy, corn, vegetable, or safflower. Olive oil is the healthiest oil, but it does not have "neutral" impact – that is, it has a very unique and powerful flavor. In many dishes, you can use olive oil for sautéing vegetables. But it is not recommended to use olive oil in batters or doughs because the flavor can be overwhelming. The recipes generally indicate when a "neutral" oil is needed. Where it is not specified, you can use any oil.

Spices

Spices are everything in Indian cooking. That means they sometimes require some endeavor and dedication. Indian spices are not just powders in a store-bought bottle. They are often seeds that need to be ground or dry roasted or fried – or a combination of all three. They are sometimes leaves that need to be plucked and cleaned and finely diced. This can be laborious and time-consuming, but the result is a wash of aroma that is unlike anything experienced in a standard western kitchen.

There are several ways to grind spices. By hand, you can use a mortar and pestle, or something called a "shil noda" which is a board and rolling pin especially for grinding spices. You can also use the western "chef's method", in which you place the seeds on a sheet of baking paper, fold it over, place the chef's knife flat on top of the paper, and then lean in to the knife using all your weight, again and again, until it is all crushed. Alternatively, you can make your life easier and purchase a coffee grinder and use it solely for the spices. (If you do use it for coffee, make sure you clean it out well before using it for spices to avoid adding a coffee flavor to a recipe.)

At the risk of sounding heretical, I will also say that there are times when you can reach for the store-bought powder without too much damage. Ground coriander, cardamom and cumin are available and flavorful. Certainly, there is something very special about the potent aroma of fresh leaves and seeds. But that can be balanced against issues of time and labor. In any case, the coffee grinder is the best time-saver for busy cooks, although, to be honest, I love my mortar and pestle.

Also, you may be wondering, how "hot" is "hot" when we label each of the recipes. We use a scale of spiciness here to describe the dishes – from mild to moderate to spicy to very hot. But these terms are very subjective. (There is a Hebrew expression al ta'am vare'ach eyn l'hitvake'ach – you can't argue about taste and smell). One person's mild is another person's grab-that-pitcher-of-water. And Indian cooking assumes a certain baseline of spiciness. No self-respecting Indian would eat plain rice the way Americans do. It is simply not considered a real food if it doesn't have some flavor. So these labels are only guidelines. My advice is to trust your own palate. And remember, if you want to cut down on the spiciness, you can always exclude the chilis.

Hard to find ingredients

There are some components of Indian cooking that are hard to find in average supermarkets outside of India. Look for local Indian shops or shop online for the ingredients you need. You can also try and make some yourself. In other cases, you can try to find replacements for some of the ingredients. For instance, if you can't find paneer ("curd", or white cheese), you can substitute a very easy (and cheap) item that is included in this list below.

Here are a few suggestions for substitutions:

Amchoor (mango powder)	Use lemon juice, lime juice or citric acid
Fresh coconut	Use ground coconut or coconut flakes
Jaggery (sugarcane pulp)	Use brown sugar, maple syrup or molasses – use half the amount of sugar since it is sweeter than jaggery
Paneer	Use ricotta, cottage cheese, farmer cheese, or yogurt

Careful with the chilis!

DO NOT use a knife on a chili pepper until you have firmly put on your glove! It will lead to a very unpleasant condition called "hot chili hands", which is exactly what it sounds like. Your hands will burn up and you will bounce around in hot unhappiness.

There are many supposed remedies for this situation – yogurt, baking soda, dishwashing liquid, and coconut oil. But to be honest coming from experience, none of them really work too well. The bottom line is, it takes a few hours of suffering and then it passes, and better to avoid altogether. And remember, if you've used chopped fresh chili peppers in dough, I recommend kneading that dough with gloves on your hands as well.

While we are on the subject of chilis, note that the size of Indian chilis is different from the size of chilis in other places in the world. Indians use very small chilis, around one inch long, whereas elsewhere a chili can be 4-5 inches long. So when a recipe calls for "two small chilis", consider that this is an Indian size.

Conversions and measurements

Speaking of variations in size, measuring ingredients is more complicated than it seems. There are three primary ways to measure ingredients in recipes.

1. **Volume.** This is the standard method in American recipes, as in "1 cup of flour", or "2 tablespoons of oil. However, it gets complicated because of UK versus US measurements. In addition, there can be a certain lack of precision depending on how packed the flour is, or how finely diced the vegetables in the cup are.

2. **Weight.** This is the standard in UK and Indian recipes, as in "250 grams of flour". This creates more uniformity in measuring, for sure, because there is no variation based on how densely a cup is packed and this can be solved by owning a kitchen scale. It also requires attention to the exact weights of every item in every recipe. Items will vary, for example, between 1 cup of flour versus one cup of feathers, which obviously have vastly different weights. There is even variation in weight between sugar and flour. Still, there is value to that kind of precision for many people, especially in the area of baking, that is more of a science than an art.

3. **Visual description.** "Three medium onions" is the most natural way that most people measure their ingredients in real life. This is the easiest but also the most non-standard form of measurement. One person's "medium" onion is another person's "large".

In this book, we are consistent in our inconsistency! We go back and forth between these different descriptions and measurements. This is in part because there are over 16 different contributors and each one used her own system. Trying to create consistency between all of them was a nearly impossible task, and we decided not to convert the recipes using one uniform system in order to reflect the diversity of this entire project.

However, to try and make this easier, we are including here some useful conversion charts that compare US and UK measures of weight, volume and temperature, as well as conversions between weight and volume of some key ingredients. These charts are culled from various useful sources, including Allrecipes.com, IndiaCurry.com, The Metric Kitchen, and Errenskitchen.com.

UK-US liquid volume conversions

½ teaspoon	⅙ tablespoon	1/16 ounce	2.5 milliliters
1 teaspoon	⅓ tablespoon	⅛ ounce	5 milliliters
½ tablespoon	1 ½ teaspoons	¼ fluid ounce	7.5 milliliters
1 tablespoon	3 teaspoons	½ fluid ounce	15 milliliters
2 tablespoons	⅛ cup	1 fluid ounce	30 milliliters
3 tablespoons	⅙ cup	1 ½ fluid ounces	45 milliliters
¼ cup	4 tablespoons	2 fluid ounces	60 milliliters
⅓ cup	5 tablespoons + 1 teaspoon	2 ⅓ fluid ounces	80 milliliters
½ cup	8 tablespoons	4 fluid ounces	120 milliliters
¾ cup	12 tablespoons	6 fluid ounces	177 milliliters
1 cup	16 tablespoons	8 fluid oz. (½ pint)	237 milliliters
1 pint	2 cups	16 fluid ounces	.47 liters
1 quart	4 cups/ 2 pints	32 fluid ounces	.95 liters
1 gallon	16 cups/ 4 quarts	128 fluid ounces	3.8 liters

UK-US weight conversions

453.6 grams	16 ounces/ 1 pound
1 gram	0.035 ounce
28 grams	1 ounce
100 grams	3.5 ounces
224 grams	8 ounces/ 1 cup
1 kilogram (kg)	35 ounces/2.205 pounds

UK-US length measurements

1 inch	2.54 centimeters
1/16 inch	1.5875 millimeters
0.3937 inch	1 centimeter
3.28 feet	1 meter

UK-US temperature conversion

Convert °F to °C (Fahrenheit-32)x(0.556)
Convert °C to °F (Celsius)x1.8+32

Freezing Point for Water	32°F	0°C
Boiling Point for Water	212°F	100°C
Room Temperature	68°F	20°C
Baking Temperature	350°F	177°C
Fryer Temperature	350°F	177°C
Refrigerator	40°F	4.5°C

Weight to volume conversions of key ingredients

Butter

¼ cup of Butter	57 grams
⅓ cup of Butter	76 grams
½ cup of Butter	113 grams
1 cup of Butter	227 grams

All-purpose flour (maida) and confectioners' sugar

⅛ cup (2 Tbsp)	16 grams	.563 ounce
¼ cup	32 grams	1.13 ounces
⅓ cup	43 grams	1.5 ounces
½ cup	64 grams	2.25 ounces
1 cup	128 grams	4.5 ounces

Rice

⅛ cup	25 grams	1 ounce
¼ cup	50 grams	1.5 ounces
⅓ cup	66 grams	2.25 ounces
½ cup	100 grams	3.5 ounces
1 cup	200 grams	7 ounces

White sugar (granulated)

⅛ cup	12.5 grams	.44 ounce
¼ cup	25 grams	.88 ounce
⅓ cup	33 grams	1 ounce
½ cup	50 grams	1.7 ounces
1 cup	100 grams	3.5 ounces

Coconut flakes

2 tbsp	25 grams	.89 ounce
¼ cup	50 grams	1.78 ounces
⅓ cup	67 grams	2.37 ounces
½ cup	100 grams	3.55 ounces
1 cup	201 grams	7.1 ounces

Here is a useful chart of some other items, from a website called "The Metric Kitchen":

	1 cup	¾ cup	⅔ cup	½ cup	⅓ cup	¼ cup	2 Tbsp
Brown sugar, packed firmly	180 gr	135 gr	120 gr	90 gr	60 gr	45 gr	23 gr
Corn flour	160 gr	120 gr	100 gr	80 gr	50 gr	40 gr	20 gr
Macaroni, uncooked	140 gr	100 gr	90 gr	70 gr	45 gr	35 gr	17 gr
Couscous, uncooked	180 gr	135 gr	120 gr	90 gr	60 gr	45 gr	22 gr
Oats, uncooked	90 gr	65 gr	60 gr	45 gr	30 gr	22 gr	11 gr
Table salt	300 gr	230 gr	200 gr	150 gr	100 gr	75 gr	40 gr
Chopped fruit and vegetables	150 gr	110 gr	100 gr	75 gr	50 gr	40 gr	20 gr
Nuts, chopped	150 gr	110 gr	100 gr	75 gr	50 gr	40 gr	20 gr
Nuts, ground	120 gr	90 gr	80 gr	60 gr	40 gr	30 gr	15 gr
Bread crumbs, dry	150 gr	110 gr	100 gr	75 gr	50 gr	40 gr	20 gr
Parmesan cheese, grated	90 gr	65 gr	60 gr	45 gr	30 gr	22 gr	11 gr

Key to symbols

 Indicates the serving size the recipe yields.

 Indicates the recipe is vegan.

 Indicates the recipe is gluten-free.

 Indicates the recipe is dairy.

 Indicates the recipe has an allergen such as nuts, coconut, eggs, or sesame seeds.

 Indicates how much preparation time is needed for the recipe.

 Indicates how much cooking time is needed for the recipe.

 Indicates how much advanced preparation time is needed, such as soaking beans overnight or letting dough rise.

 Indicates the recipe requires special cooking equipment.

 Indicates the level of difficulty of the recipe with 1-3 chef hats.

 Indicates the level of spiciness of the recipe with 1-3 chili peppers.

 Indicates the level of sweetness of the recipe with 1-3 honey dippers.

glossary:
on language and culture

A note about spelling: In translating from Hindi or Marathi to English, there is often no correct spelling. When do we use the "h"? Is it "w" or "v"? Do we double the "a" for accurate pronunciations, despite its awkwardness in English? Is it a "d" or an "r"? These questions arise for many of the most common words. For instance: Dal or dahl? Puri or poori? Tawa or Tava? Pulao, pulav or pulaw? Badam or badaam? Bhaji or bhajji? Puja, pujah, or poojah? Pakora or pakoda? You get the picture. It is a copywriter's nightmare.

The reason for this of course is it is about language – and India has hundreds of different languages with so many different sounds. There is one sound in Hindi that uses a click of the tongue on the roof of the mouth that is somewhere between the English "d" and "r". In transferring the words into English, it can go either way – hence pakora and pakoda. They are the same word, but reflect different evolutions and linguistic migrations.

There is also the issue of combined words. Indians often combine a string of words into one word. These are cultures of language. The dish Medu Wadi, for example – also spelled vadi or vada or wada – as one word or two. Indians tend to simply call it "meduwadi", but a native English speaker will likely hear it as two words. "Medu" is a Kannada word that means "soft" and "wadi" is the common Hindi word that means "fritter". But most people don't even know or care about the origin of the name of this popular snack. It's just meduwadi. So, one word or two? There is no satisfactory or even correct answer.

I wanted consistency in spelling, but I discovered that it is not possible to be both consistent and loyal to the culture. In this list, I have tried to include a variety of spellings to cover all the bases, but the process is a bit of a bottomless pit. I take it as a lesson in finding my inner shanti, despite my perfectionist editing inclinations.

Also note that some items appear in both their Hindi and Marathi forms. This intermingling of Marathi, Hindi and English – as well as occasional references from Sanskrit and other languages – reflects the reality of everyday communication in Mumbai. This is the language.

Aam	mangoes
Aam panha/kairee	green (unripe) mangoes
Adrak	fresh ginger
Agarbatti	incense stick
Ajwain	carom seed
Aloo	potato
Alu	taro leaves
Amchoor/amchur	dried mango powder
Amjud	celery
Amla	Indian gooseberry
Anar-daana	pomegranate seeds
Anda	egg
Appe	dumpling
Asafoetida	hing, a tree sap fried and crumbled to powder
Atta	whole wheat flour
Badaam	almonds
Batata	potatoes
Belan	thin rolling pin
Besan	gram flour made from ground chickpeas
Bhaji	dry vegetable stew
Bhajji	fried balls of dough
Bharwa	stuffed
Bhatma	soya beans
Bhindi	okra
Bindi	ceremonial red powder-based dot placed on the forehead for ritual purposes
Brinjal	eggplant
Burfi/burfee/barfi	diamond-shaped cake from reduced milk and chickpea flour
Chakki	hand operated stone mill to grind grains to make flour
Chakla	stone rolling board
Chakra phool	star anise
Chana	chickpea
Chapatti	flatbread
Chai	tea
Chana dal	split back chickpeas
Chawal	rice
Chawal ka atta	rice flour
Chenna	type of cheese
Chikki	nut brittle
Dahl or dal	lentils

introductions

Dalchini	cinnamon
Dhania	coriander
Dhirde	pancake
Dosa	rice flour-based flatbread
Dudhi	pumpkin or bottle gourd
Elaichi (bari/choti)	cardamom (black/green)
Fullower	cauliflower
Gaajar	carrot
Ganesh	Hindu god of good fortune, "elephant-head" god
Garam masala	classic Indian spice mixture
Ghavan	rice flour flatbread
Goal mirch	peppercorn
Gulab	rose
Gulab jal	rose water
Haldi	turmeric
Halwa	sweet dessert
Hing/asafetida	tree sap fried and crumbled to powder
Idli	spicy, soft, steamed doughy balls eaten as snacks
Imli	tamarind
Jaggery	sugarcane pulp
Jal jeera	spice mixture used for digestion drink
Jaifal/jaiphal	nutmeg
Jeera	cumin seed
Jhaara	flat, slotted spatula for deep frying
Jowar	sorghum flour
Jhungori	millet
Kachori	deep-fried sweet snack with a sweet topping
Kadai/karahi/karai	big earthenware or steel pot with handles on each side, also called an Indian wok
Kadhi	gravy or soup-like thick liquid dish
Kairee	unripened mangoes
Kajoo	cashews
Kala namak/sanchal	black rock salt
Kamarkas	sage
kanda	onion
Kari patta/meetha neem patta	curry leaf
Karwande	Indian berry
kasuri methi	dried fenugreek leaves
Katori	small curry bowl
Kesar/zaafraan	saffron
Kheer	rice pudding
Kheera	cucumber
Khichree/khichdy	rice and beans cooked together
Khoya/khawa/mava	dried milk
Kuskus	poppy seeds

Kokum	Garcinia indica fruit, native to Maharashtra
Kothimbir	coriander
Khumbi	mushrooms
Ladoo	sweet dessert balls
Lakshmi	Hindu goddess of wealth
Lassi	yogurt-based drink
Lassun	fresh garlic
Laung/lavang	cloves
Limbu	cardamom
Lonche	pickled vegetables
Maida	all-purpose wheat flour (white)
Masala	spice
Masala dabba	spice box
Masala dosa	classic Indian spice mix
Masoor	lentils
Mattar	peas
Mattar dal	split peas
Maval petals	cock's comb, used for yellow-red coloring
Methi	fenugreek seeds
Methi, hari	fresh fenugreek leaves
Methi, kasoori	dried fenugreek leaves
Mirch, degi	paprika
Mirch, kali	ground black pepper
Mirch, lal	red chili pepper
Mirch, hari	fresh green chili pepper
Moong dahl/dal	yellow split peas or lentils
Mulathi/jethi-madh	licorice root
Murabha/murabba	sweet fruit-based preserve
Mysore	semolina
Naan	wheat-based flatbread
Naarial khopra	coconut
Nimboo/nimbu	lime
Nimboo phool	citric acid
Namak	salt
Paalak/palak	spinach
Paani	water
Pakoda/pakora	dumplings made of vegetables or cheese, wrapped in dough and deep fried
Paneer	white curded cheese
Paniyaram	pan for making appes
Paratha	griddle-fried soft flatbread, often stuffed with vegetables
Pippali	long pepper
Pista	pistachio nuts
Podina	fresh peppermint leaves
Poha	flattened rice flakes that are mixed with water

Prasad	an offering of sweets and treats on a thali (tin) used in pujah rituals
Pujah/pooja/puja	rituals performed at home or in everyday places away from the temples
Pulav/pulaw/pulao	rice cooked with spices
Puri/poori	deep-fried flatbread
Rai	black mustard seeds
Rai, kuria	cracked black mustard seeds
Rajgira	amaranth
Rajgira ka atta	amaranth flour
Ratan Jot	alkanet root, used as a red powder dye
Rava/rawa/sooji	semolina
Roti	basic whole wheat unleavened flat bread
Raita	cold yogurt dip
Rana	grated fresh coconut
Rassa	stew or gravy
Saboo/subadhana	tapioca
Samosa	triangle-shaped stuffed and fried dough
Sari	traditional Indian women's dress, consisting of a long garment wrapped around the body, and a tunic that usually reveals the midriff
Sarson	mustard seeds
Saunf	anise
Saunf, moti	fennel seed
Shakahari	vegetarian
Sharbat	juice
Shepu/soa	dill
Shil noda/sil batta	flat black stone and triangular stone or rolling pin for grinding spices
Simla mirch	bell pepper (capsicum)
Sirka	vinegar
Sooji/rava/rawa	semolina
Sabudana/saboo	tapioca
Tawa or tava	flat iron griddle for making bread
Tej patta	bay leaf
Thali	round tin platter for serving a complete meal, or used in pujah rituals
Tika	red powder placed on the forehead for ritual purposes (also bindi)
Tikki	minced food patty
Til	sesame seeds
Tokani	brass water pitcher
Tulsi	basil
Upvas	fasting foods
Urad	black beans
Uttapam	thick pancake with toppings
Vadi/wadi	fried dough ball filled with spices

introductions

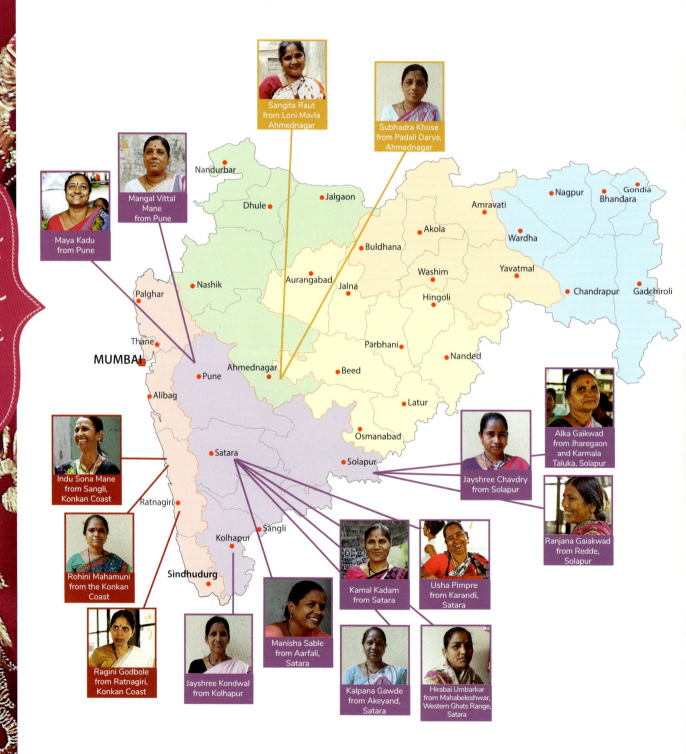

Indian cooking has many unique components, some of which require advance preparation. Items such as ghee, garam masala, and paneer are a must. This section will help you set the stage for preparing a fantastic Maharashtrian meal.

getting started

Ghee
Ginger-Garlic Paste
Garam Masala
Paneer
Rice
Classic Chapattis

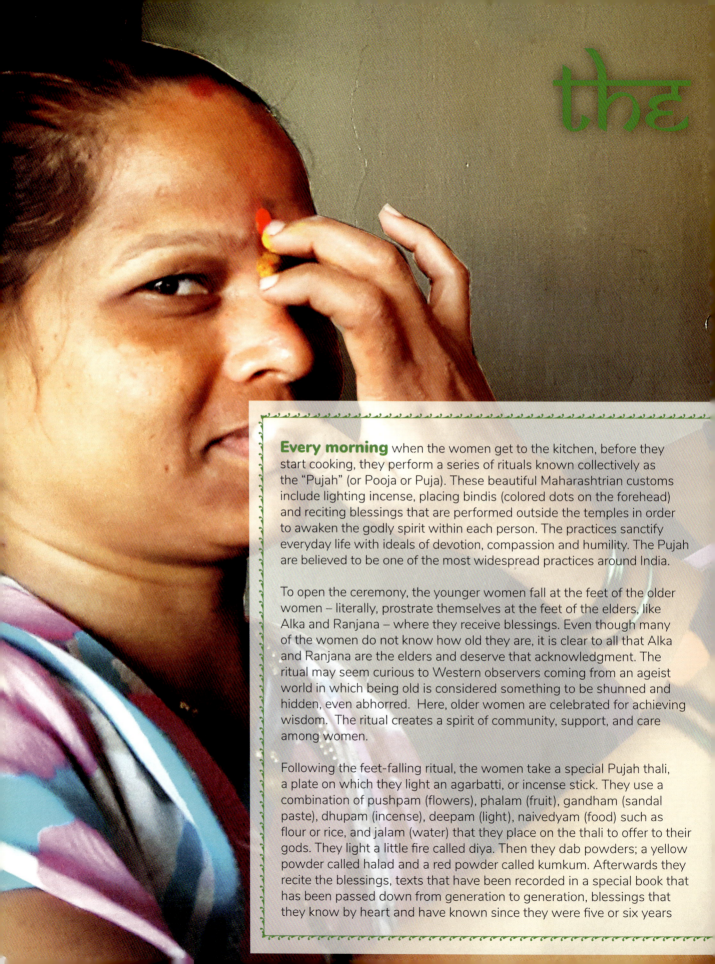

the

Every morning when the women get to the kitchen, before they start cooking, they perform a series of rituals known collectively as the "Pujah" (or Pooja or Puja). These beautiful Maharashtrian customs include lighting incense, placing bindis (colored dots on the forehead) and reciting blessings that are performed outside the temples in order to awaken the godly spirit within each person. The practices sanctify everyday life with ideals of devotion, compassion and humility. The Pujah are believed to be one of the most widespread practices around India.

To open the ceremony, the younger women fall at the feet of the older women – literally, prostrate themselves at the feet of the elders, like Alka and Ranjana – where they receive blessings. Even though many of the women do not know how old they are, it is clear to all that Alka and Ranjana are the elders and deserve that acknowledgment. The ritual may seem curious to Western observers coming from an ageist world in which being old is considered something to be shunned and hidden, even abhorred. Here, older women are celebrated for achieving wisdom. The ritual creates a spirit of community, support, and care among women.

Following the feet-falling ritual, the women take a special Pujah thali, a plate on which they light an agarbatti, or incense stick. They use a combination of pushpam (flowers), phalam (fruit), gandham (sandal paste), dhupam (incense), deepam (light), naivedyam (food) such as flour or rice, and jalam (water) that they place on the thali to offer to their gods. They light a little fire called diya. Then they dab powders; a yellow powder called halad and a red powder called kumkum. Afterwards they recite the blessings, texts that have been recorded in a special book that has been passed down from generation to generation, blessings that they know by heart and have known since they were five or six years

pujah

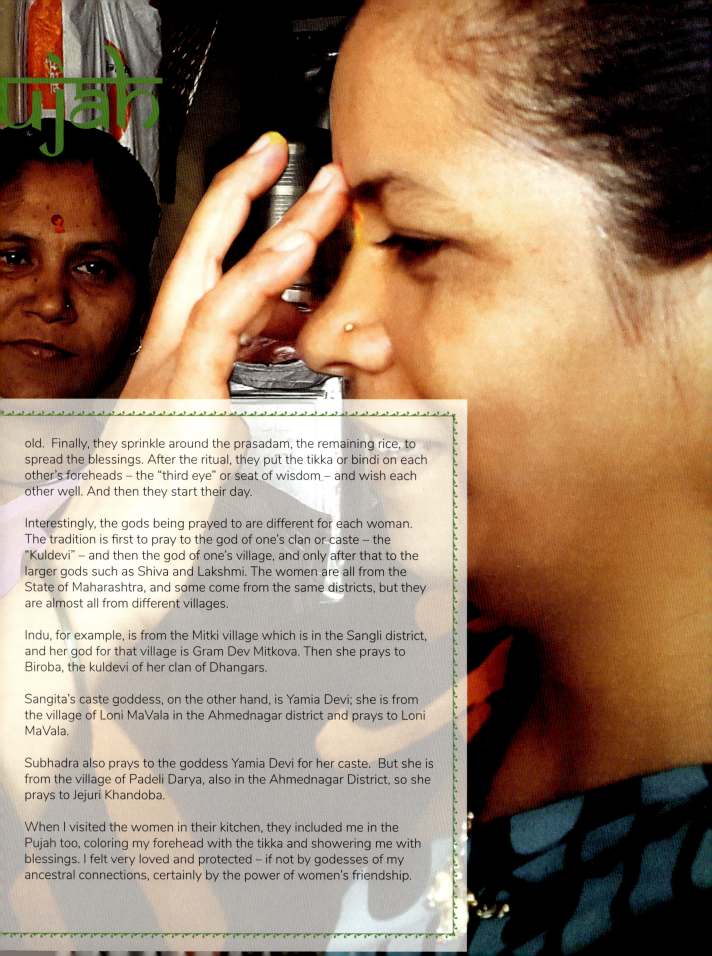

old. Finally, they sprinkle around the prasadam, the remaining rice, to spread the blessings. After the ritual, they put the tikka or bindi on each other's foreheads – the "third eye" or seat of wisdom – and wish each other well. And then they start their day.

Interestingly, the gods being prayed to are different for each woman. The tradition is first to pray to the god of one's clan or caste – the "Kuldevi" – and then the god of one's village, and only after that to the larger gods such as Shiva and Lakshmi. The women are all from the State of Maharashtra, and some come from the same districts, but they are almost all from different villages.

Indu, for example, is from the Mitki village which is in the Sangli district, and her god for that village is Gram Dev Mitkova. Then she prays to Biroba, the kuldevi of her clan of Dhangars.

Sangita's caste goddess, on the other hand, is Yamia Devi; she is from the village of Loni MaVala in the Ahmednagar district and prays to Loni MaVala.

Subhadra also prays to the goddess Yamia Devi for her caste. But she is from the village of Padeli Darya, also in the Ahmednagar District, so she prays to Jejuri Khandoba.

When I visited the women in their kitchen, they included me in the Pujah too, coloring my forehead with the tikka and showering me with blessings. I felt very loved and protected – if not by godesses of my ancestral connections, certainly by the power of women's friendship.

Clarified Butter

This Indian clarified butter, full of health benefits and a sweet aroma, is a staple in every Indian kitchen. Suitable for people who are lactose intolerant, ghee improves digestion and reduces inflammation in the body. The method for preparing ghee is both very simple and yet also tricky. It takes only around 15 minutes, but learning to recognize the stages of the clarification process and when to turn off the heat can take practice. Also, it is very important to use unsalted butter since salt can negatively affect the process. Water also has a damaging effect, so make sure that everything coming into contact with the butter during the process – every spoon, pot and strainer – is completely dry.

Ingredients

2 sticks/ 226 gr salt-free butter

Method

1. Cut the butter into pieces and place in a dry saucepan.

2. Heat the butter over a medium heat until completely melted.

3. Simmer for 10-15 minutes. The ghee will go through several changes. You will be able to hear it crackling as the top layer changes form. When the crackling dies down and you see a layer of white foam on top, a middle layer of bright golden oil, and a layer of brown milk solids at the bottom of the pan, you will know that it is done. Do not stir it or stick a spoon in it while it is simmering. Just let it keep going. And do not add any water at any point. It will be a yellowish-brown bubbling liquid.

4. Wait a few moments for it to cool. Skim all of the foam off the top layer with a spoon and pour the remaining liquid through a wire mesh strainer lined with cheesecloth or gauze.

5. Transfer to a clean glass jar. It will harden a bit and become the texture of shortening. Store at room temperature and it can last for months.

getting started

yields 1 cup

1 min

15-20 min

small strainer and cheese cloth

getting started

ginger-garlic paste

This paste is an essential ingredient in a wide range of dishes from snacks to mains and chutneys. With a strong aroma, using a paste speeds up the prep by eliminating some of the fine dicing. You can alter the quantities in this recipe as long as there is an even amount of garlic and ginger.

In this recipe, we included turmeric both for the flavor and color. Also, turmeric and vinegar are ingredients that kill germs and help the paste last longer. Without the vinegar, it will last a few days to a week in the refrigerator; with the vinegar, it should last 2-3 months or longer in the freezer. If you freeze the paste, best to freeze in small quantities in small ice cube trays so that you can take out a serving for each recipe you need.

Ingredients

1 cup/ 240 ml garlic cloves, minced

1 cup/ 240 ml peeled ginger, minced

1 tsp/ 5 ml turmeric (optional)

¼ cup/ 60 ml water

1 tsp/ 5 ml neutral oil (e.g., sunflower, soy, or canola)

1 tsp/ 5 ml vinegar

pinch of salt

Method

1. Place all the ingredients in a blender or food processor and blend until it becomes a paste. You may adjust the amount of water to get the right consistency of paste.

2. Transfer to an airtight jar or Ziplock bag and store in the refrigerator.

> **TIP:** Make sure the garlic and ginger are completely dry before you grind them. They will keep for longer.

> **TIP:** You can also make pastes mixing up ginger and garlic in different combinations with other flavors like onions, coriander, parsley, chili peppers, or spring onions.

> **TIP:** You can also make cashew paste, almond paste, and almost any variation, especially with seasonings that you use frequently. The method is always the same: blend your ingredients in a food processor with a little bit of oil to turn it into a paste and then keep in a jar in the refrigerator for easy use. We encourage you to experiment!

yields 1 cup

10 min

food processor or coffee grinder

getting started

Garam Masala

Spice Mix

Garam Masala is considered the go-to flavoring in India. However, each state and region in India includes different ingredients in their masalas, depending on the agriculture and history. Gujaratis, for example, use cooling coconut in their masalas, while Keralans use mace and fennel seeds. There is also something of a dispute among Maharashtrians about the use of oil in making the masala. Some people dry roast all the ingredients – which can be done over the stove for a few minutes or directly in sunlight for a few days – while others fry seeds in hot oil, especially mustard and cumin seeds. There is no one rule about what goes into the garam masala, and there are many variations. The women of the collective bring different versions to the table, and this recipe is something of a composite. It can be adjusted, of course, according to your own tastes and experiences.

Ingredients

- ½ cup/ 120 ml coriander seeds
- 10-15 cloves
- 4-5 cinnamon sticks or ¼ cup/ 60 ml powdered cinnamon
- 2 Tbsp/ 30 ml cumin seeds (jeera)
- 2 Tbsp/ 30 ml caraway seeds
- 2 Tbsp/ 30 ml mustard seeds
- 1 Tbsp/ 15 ml fenugreek seeds (methi)
- 10-15 black peppercorns
- 10 black and 5 green cardamom pods or 1 tsp cardamom powder
- 2 nutmegs grated, or ½ tsp/ 2.5 ml powdered nutmeg
- ½ tsp/ 2.5 ml anise seeds
- 1 tsp/ 5 ml turmeric

Method

1. Dry roast all the seed ingredients. Anything you are using in whole seed form and not powder form you can dry roast using one of two methods. Either place the seeds in a dry frying pan over a low heat for 3-4 minutes until they brown, or lay them out on a baking sheet and let it sit in the sun for 1-2 days for the same effect.

2. When the mixture is cool, blend with the powdered ingredients and crush into powder form. You can do this in one of a few ways: either electrically using a blender, food processor, or coffee grinder, or manually using a mortar and pestle. You can also use a "shil noda", a stone slab and roller, which is a traditional method going back many generations.

One other option is to use the Western "chef's method", as follows: lay out a sheet of baking paper and pour your mixture onto half the paper. Then, fold the other half over the paper and lay a large chef's knife horizontally on top of the paper, pressing down on the chef's knife, and leaning down with all your strength until everything is crushed into a powder.

3. Whichever method you use, you should have a nice pile of powdered, aromatic spice that is consistent in texture and color. Store in an air-tight jar; the mixture can easily keep for a year. You can also double or triple the recipe to make a larger quantity.

yields 1 cup

15 min

15 min or 1-2 days

mortar and pestle, coffee grinder

getting started

White Cheese

This mild white cheese, something in between cottage cheese, ricotta, and feta, is a staple of the Maharashtrian diet. It forms the basis or the stuffing of many dishes, including masalas, parathas, pakoras, and more. In some parts of the world it is hard to find classic Indian paneer. If you can't get paneer, you can either use an alternative white cheese – such as farmer cheese, yogurt or ricotta for curries, or halumi for pakoras – or else you can make it with this recipe! It is not a difficult process, and is a great skill to add to your kitchen set.

Ingredients

2 quarts/ 2 liters whole milk (at least 3% fat; long life milk cannot be used)

¼ cup/ 120 ml vinegar or lemon juice

salt to taste

Method

1. Pour the milk into a large, heavy pot. Heat it on a low to medium flame, to slowly come to a boil. It is very important not to rush this part because you don't want the milk to burn. Stir occasionally to bring out some frothiness.

2. When it is just boiled, pour in the vinegar or lemon juice. Stir for a minute, preferably with a wooden spoon, and then turn off the heat. You should see the milk begin to separate between the "curds" and the "whey". The curds are the solids and the whey is the liquid. If it doesn't start happening, add a bit more vinegar or lemon juice, but not too much because you don't want it to overwhelm the taste. Continue stirring gently for 2-3 minutes to make sure that the process of separation happens. After around 5 minutes of stirring, cover the pot and let it rest for 30-45 minutes. (You can wait less time, but the paneer may be too hot to handle in the next steps.)

3. Prepare to separate the curds and whey. Place a colander or sieve into a large bowl inside the basin. Take a large piece of cheesecloth (or, you can use a very thin white fabric that you can buy in any fabric store, around half a meter or half a yard will do the trick), and lay it out on top of the colander.

4. When the milk has settled a bit, pour it slowly and gently into the colander over the cloth. The solids should remain in the cloth while the bowl underneath fills with the liquid whey. If you used lemon juice and not vinegar in the process, take a moment to rinse the paneer in the colander so it will not have a lemony tang to it.

yields 2-3 cups

1.5 hours

20-30 min

cheese cloth, sieve

5. Pull the cloth around the curd, and then slowly lift the cloth to let the liquid drain out. Squeeze the liquid into the bowl, as much as you can. Then place your new block of paneer onto a plate to shape it into a rounded flat mass. Continue squeezing out the liquid until it forms a solid mass on the plate.

6. Now wrap the paneer up again in order to let it dry and settle into its shape. You can do this in one of two ways, or use both ways one after another. The first method is to put something heavy on top of the plate, like a heavy pot or jar filled with lentils, and let it sit on the paneer for an hour. That will get it flat and solid. The second method – which you can do after 15-minutes of using the first method or do on its own – is to hang the paneer, tied up in the cloth, over a sink so it can drip into the drain.

7. When the paneer is nice and firm, open it up on a plate, and cut into cubes. It should be firm and a bit crumbly. And delicious. Store your paneer cubes in an airtight container in the fridge. It should keep well up to a week.

getting started

Rice

Although rice is the foundation of the Maharashtrian meal, it is never eaten alone. It is more like the canvas on which you put all kinds of colors and flavors – curries, dal, sambars or kadhis. Many meals incorporate spiced-up rice – or "pilaf" or "pulav" – and cook it with vegetables or lentils for a one pot meal. There are several views on how to prepare rice.

One way to prepare rice is to measure the water precisely so that the rice will soak up all the liquid at the exact moment when it is ready, with the perfect stickiness in its texture. Another method which is preferred among many Maharashtrian women is to prepare the rice like pasta, boiling a pot of water, pouring in rice, and then draining out the water when the rice is done. Personally, I prefer the taste of the rice that soaks up all the water. It is also the method used for spiced-up rice because you cannot drain spiced rice without losing the flavor. But Maharashtrian women have some interesting reasons for the colander method, including cosmetic and health uses for the discarded water. We present both of these methods here.

Ingredients

1 cup/ 240 ml basmati rice

pinch of salt and pepper

½ tsp/ 2.5 ml cardamom powder (optional)

2-3 whole star anise seeds (optional)

Method

1. Prepare the rice by pouring it into a big bowl, covering it with cold water, or running water over it while rubbing your fingers over the grains to remove rocks and dirt. This process is important because it both cleans the grains and removes excess starch, making the rice less sticky and easier to digest. Rinse the rice one last time. When you're done, drain the excess water, and then soak the rice in fresh water for 15-20 minutes.

2. Cook the rice using one of the methods below.

Option 1: Straining

Bring 4-5 cups of water to boil in a pot, with a pinch of salt. Next pour in the rice and cook uncovered for 5-10 minutes on a medium flame. You should be able to see the rice grains rising to the top and moving vigorously with the water. When the rice is done, that movement subsides, and the cooking liquid becomes whitish in color. To check if it is done, scoop out a few grains with a spoon and press them between your thumb and forefinger to make sure that it is soft. Drain the cooked rice using a colander the way you would drain pasta.

getting started

4 servings

30 min

15 min

Option 2: Absorbing

Pour the rice into a pot, and pour over it two cups of cold water. Add salt and pepper (and any other spices you'd like, such as cardamom or anise), cover the pot, and bring to a rapid boil. Reduce heat to a low flame for 8-10 minutes and cook until the water is absorbed. Best not to repeatedly check on the rice as it needs the steam to cook.

Fluff with a fork to make sure the grains are separate, soft and thin. This is not "sticky rice" that is popular in other Asian countries, but separate-grain rice.

Great rice with curries or other entrees, or use as the basis for stuffing. Best served hot, but can be reheated.

> **TIP:** If you are using the straining method, collect the water. This is "Rice Water" and it is believed to have health benefits and is often served to people who are sick or elderly. Indian women also use this to starch their saris and to wash their hair instead of shampoo.

> **TIP:** If you are using the absorbing method, usually white rice needs 2 cups of water for every cup of rice whereas brown rice uses a three-to-one ratio of water to rice. However, if you've soaked the rice, then subtract 2-3 tablespoons of water per cup of rice because the grains have already absorbed some water.

> **TIP:** Rice expands by three when it is cooked, so plan your meals accordingly.

Classic Chapattis

Soft Indian Flatbread

The chapatti forms the center of many Indian meals. Like in many cultures, the bread in Indian culture is used like a brush, sponge, or a palate. It is the backdrop of the meal, or at times an instrument to soak up and enjoy the wide variety of dips, curries, chutneys, and dals that Indian cuisine has to offer. Chapattis are relatively simple foods that can be quickly cooked on a non-stick frying pan, although it can be helpful to have a "tawa" or flat griddle frying pan specially designed for chapattis. If you don't have a tawa, a regular frying pan is just as effective. Also, you can adjust the proportions of white flour to whole wheat flour according to your own tastes.

getting started

Ingredients

1 cup/ 240 ml all-purpose white flour or durum wheat flour (atta)

1 cup/ 240 ml whole wheat flour

1 tsp/ 5 ml salt

2/ 30 ml Tbsp oil or ghee

¾ cup/ 177 ml warm water or more as needed

Method

1. In a large bowl, stir together the all-purpose flour, whole wheat flour, and salt. Stir in the oil or ghee. Using ghee is preferred, but you can use any oil just as effectively. Gradually add water as you knead. The dough should be soft and elastic but not sticky. Knead well for around ten minutes so that the gluten that is naturally contained in the dough is activated.

2. Place the dough into an oiled bowl, cover with a damp cloth, and let it rest for half an hour.

3. When the dough is ready, form golf ball-sized balls. As you remove each ball from the bowl, keep the rest of the dough covered so it retains its moisture. You should have around 10-12 balls from this batch.

4. Heat a lightly greased tawa or small frying pan until it is very hot. While it is heating up, begin rolling out the balls of dough into flat discs, like tortillas. Place the chapatti onto the heated tawa for around one minute per side, until the underside gets brown bubbles on it. Flip it over to the other side and watch it puff up. You can burst the "bubbles" that form or leave them to relax themselves. Remove the flipped chapattis after one minute.

Best served immediately, with any dish, topping, or sandwich filling of your choice.

10-12 servings

40 min

20 min

Thin rolling pin (belan) and flat griddle (tawa)

getting started

sustaining children at the love2learn school

257,400 meals

That is how many meals the women make every year as part of the Eat2Learn program providing meals for children in school.

1000 children

That is how many children ages 6-16 are learning at the GPM Love2Learn school in the urban Kalwa slum in Thane and in the remote rural tribal district of Palgar, Maharashtra, where they receive meals in school.

The children come for the food and stay for the learning. Or maybe it's the other way around. They come for the learning and stay for the food. Either way, the food has transformed the learning experience. Children and their parents know that the school is a place that looks after each child – in mind, body and spirit. Thanks to the women's cooking, children are eating well – and they are learning. They are loved and tended by all around.

The food is made fresh every morning out of local ingredients like lentils, pulses and vegetables. The children look forward to the food, and they eat it with joy, satisfaction and gusto., because they know that the food is made with love and care. It is about sustaining the children. And it is about looking after the community.

On Mondays the children eat poha – rice flakes with vegetables.
On Tuesdays the children eat dal khichdi – lentil and rice stew.
On Wednesdays the children eat chana dal – black bean curry.
On Thursdays the children eat veg pulav – a pilaf made with mixed vegetables.
On Fridays the children eat soya pulav – a stew made from soya chunks, an affordable and simple source of protein.
And on Saturdays, a special treat, the children eat sheet – a kind of sweet semolina pudding that they particularly love.

And for special occasions and holidays, the women prepare special holiday fare like shankarpali and modaks. Children living in conditions of poverty face many educational, medical, nutritional, developmental and financial challenges. By offering fresh, hot, nutritious meals in schools, the school is able to address many of the issues at once.

The school also uses creative pedagogy, pedagogic approaches, and student-centered learning to maximize the educational impact of the program.

"Children, you have a terrific opportunity with the Love2Learn program and GPM to expand your academic horizons, grow healthy and achieve many great things," said Dr. Raghunat Rathod, the Head of the District Government medical services, to the children. He visited the Love2Learn school and watched tribal dance performances by the children. "With the tools available to you now, you can acquire knowledge and contribute back to your village communities and the district".

Indian hosts often will not begin a meal until after drinks are served – especially cooling drinks that can keep Maharashtrian heat at bay. Favorite cooling drink ingredients include mango, cumin, and the famous kokum fruit.

drinks

Amm Panna

Mango Lassi

Cardamom Lassi

Kokum Sharbat

Limbu Sharbat

Jal Jeera

Sol Kadi

Faluda

Spices of Life

If there is one major difference between Indian cooking and western cooking, it is the role of spices. And by spices, we mean the scents, aromas, and flavors of life.

The first clue that the women of the collective cherish their spices is found in an item called a Masala Dabba. This is a round metal tin that contains a woman's favorite spices. It is almost like a cosmetics bag, that collection of personally-assembled accoutrements to one's daily life. (Actually, a lot of spices have cosmetic uses as well, but that is the subject of a different book.) The items in a woman's Masala Dabba reflect her tastes, passions, and loves; they reflect her traditions, family history, attachments, and connections to foods. The Masala Dabba is like an artist's palate, the vital tool with which she paints her kitchen, her table, and her home. It is how she shares her character to the world at large and to the world of eating and nourishment.

The Masala Dabba is also a kind of family heirloom. Choices of spices, and the methods of grinding spices, are practices that are passed down from generation to generation via the spice box – from grandmother to mother to daughter. The women have their masala "secrets" that they carry with them through the box. Women from different tribes, different villages, and different religions each hold their own knowledge through the spice box. These spices are then mixed with the food to give one's palate the taste that the ancestors have been passing down for ages. The box is like the family safe, holding its treasures.

This attitude to spices is reflected in the entire approach to cooking. A typical western-style recipe places spices last, if at all, into a recipe. A stew or soup in an American home, for example, will likely begin with some onions sautéed in oil, followed by vegetables, grains, and other items. At the end of the process, salt and pepper are added along with water, with other common spices such as parsley, basil, dill, or garlic. The flavoring process is there, but it is not the main point.

In contrast, however, Indian spices are front and center of every recipe, loud and noticed, like a maestro taking center stage. Every recipe typically begins with spices before all other ingredients – and lots of them. Many of the recipes in this cookbook, for example, call for heating mustard and cumin seeds in oil before anything else. A typical Indian recipe might have a dozen different herbs and spices, some of which may even be added twice. Many recipes call for grinding spices from their seeds, a process which may seem superfluous to western shoppers who are quite content buying powdered spices off the shelf. In Indian cooking, spices are everything. And they must be fresh. They define food. They are an entire attitude.

Spices are more than just about flavor. They reflect a relationship with the world. This generous, passionate and excited approach to spices is about recognizing the sensual bounty of the earth. It is about embracing the abundant array of colors and experiences that the ground has to offer. It is cooking with a deep connection to one's surroundings, and one's origins.

The recipes in this cookbook use ingredients that are very close to their original forms with almost no packaged foods involved in the cooking. Evolving from generations of living with close awareness of the surrounding life which is a cherished feature of Indian religious cultures, the recipes reflect not only the way the women cook, but the way they approach their relationships, and their lives. It is a deep spiritual connection to each other, and to the world in which they live.

The spice box, is the tool with which the women generously and lovingly sprinkle their passions into their food, and a beautiful reflection of a profound spiritual approach to life.

aam panna

Raw Mango Drink
by Kamal Kadam

If there is one recipe that demonstrates just how much Maharashtrians love their mangoes, it is Aam Panna, a drink made of boiled and sweetened unripe mangoes. Raw mangoes are considered a vibrant, nutrient-rich food full of Vitamin C, Vitamin B, and good for the immune system. They are also believed to help with blood diseases and gastro-intestinal issues. This recipe makes a concentrated mixture that goes a long way. If you cannot get raw mangoes in your area, you can also make the recipe with ripe mangoes, adjusting the recipe to use less sugar.

Ingredients

2-3 large raw mangoes

1 tsp/ 5 ml cardamom powder

½ tsp/ 2.5 ml black pepper

½ tsp/ 2.5 ml cumin

½ tsp/ 2.5 ml salt

1 cup/240 ml jaggery or
½ cup/ 120 ml sugar

mint leaves for garnish

Method

1. Wash mangoes and place entire fruit in a pot of water. Bring to a boil and cook until mangoes are soft, approximately 45 minutes. When they are cooked, rinse in cold water, and wait for them to cool.

2. Remove skin, discard pit, and place all the pulp into a medium-sized bowl. Add cardamom, pepper, cumin, salt and sugar or jaggery to the pulp. Mix together in a blender until smooth. Some people mix these together in a frying pan over heat for a few minutes until the sugar becomes syrupy which also gives the spices a roasted taste. Either way is fine. This is the drink concentrate.

3. To assemble the drink, use 1-2 tablespoons of concentrate per one glass of water. Serve over ice, and garnish with mint leaves.

4. Store in an airtight container in the refrigerator or freezer. It will keep for 1-2 weeks in the refrigerator, and 2-3 months in the freezer.

yields 10 cups

approx 1 hour

5 min (optional)

blender

mango lassi

Mango-Yogurt Drink
by Ragini Godhbole

The Mango Lassi is a Maharashtrian favorite. People wait all year for mango season in order to indulge in this delicious and beautiful drink. It is easy, simple, and enticingly refreshing. It can also be made with strawberries or other fruit in season.

Ingredients

1 cup/ 240 ml plain whole milk yogurt

1 cup/ 240 ml chopped ripe mango

1 Tbsp/ 5 ml sugar

1 tsp/ 5 ml ground cardamom, **plus extra** for garnish

ice

Method

1. Blend yogurt, mango, sugar and cardamom in blender for two minutes until smooth and frothy. You can adjust the amount of sugar depending on your preference and the sweetness of your mango.

2. Pour into a tall glass over ice and sprinkle with a pinch of cardamom.

2 servings   5 min

indu sona mane

Indu has always been smart. From the time she was little, everyone knew – her teachers, her parents, and the people in her village. But her family, who lived in the village of Sangli, in the Konkan region of Maharashtra, India, had different ideas that did not include investing in girls' education. They expected her, like all girls, to take care of their families, help with the household, and get married as soon as possible. And so, at the age of roughly 11, like so many of the women, Indu dropped out of school. Her teachers were devastated. One even came to Indu's house to beg her family to let her stay in school. She offered to let Indu live with her in the next village. But that was considered out of the question. Indu still gets angry talking about it, so many years later.

Today, Indu, has two children, aged 17 and 19, and she is determined to enable both children, the boy and the girl, to get as much schooling as they want.

Indu, got married at around the age of 17 – relatively late for a girl in her village – in an arranged marriage. Right after her marriage, some twenty years ago, Indu moved to Mumbai. Her husband, whom she had just met, had a job in Mumbai in the food services industry. "I had never been to Mumbai before," she says, "and I didn't know what to expect."

Life in Mumbai is different from life in the village. "In the village, our family would get together regularly and eat," she recalls with great fondness. "In the city, everyone stays in their own houses and people don't get together. In the village, we would cook together, and then we would sit together and eat. I miss that experience."

Indu has many memories of village life, especially visiting neighboring villages for fairs. Even though there are no roads between the villages

making the trek challenging, the village fairs were a highlight for her. She especially enjoyed the annual Nag Panchami festival – worshiping the snake god – which takes place every summer. "The men all take a snake and put it around them," she laughs. "It was a lot of fun."

She also remembers the food from the festivals, like the puran poli – like sweet chapattis made with gram flour – that everyone looked forward to eating. "It's a big thing in the village."

"And when mango season starts, the food becomes very exciting," she says. "You can eat the pulp with many dishes – puris, chutneys, lassis, and more."

Indu loves cooking, and she especially enjoys feeding the children. She contributed many recipes to the cookbook, including carrot halwa, bharwa bindi masala, methi poori, puran poli, pav bhaji, mango lassi, and others. Her favorite recipe is biryani.

"Being with the women is exciting," she says of the Delicio kitchen cooperative. "It is giving us a push. We are proud of that. People are coming to eat our food, to see what we are doing. We can say with pride that our food is good!"

Indu has a dream for a future: She wants to open a food stall in Kalwa in the evenings. But she wants to make sure that all the women are on board first. "Once you join hands with these women, there is no going back," she says. "There is only moving forward." But she says she can't do it alone.

cardamom lassi

Yogurt Drink
by Indu Sona Mane

When you walk into an Indian home, the first thing you are offered is a drink. Not soft-drinks or store-bought, artificially colored drinks, but rather elaborately spiced coolers full of fresh ingredients combined via methods that have been perfected over generations. One of the most popular drinks served especially, during the summer heat, are Lassis which are yogurt-based staples. This classic recipe has a cardamom flavor, making it savory rather than sweet and very refreshing.

Ingredients

1 cup/ 240 ml whole milk yogurt

¾ cup/ 177 ml whole milk

4 Tbsp/ 60 ml sugar

1 tsp/ 5 ml cardamom powder

1 tsp/ 5 ml rose water

a few strands of saffron (optional)

ice

1-2 Tbsp/ 15-30 ml chopped almonds or pistachios

yogurt or heavy cream for garnish (optional)

Method

1. Blend the yogurt and milk until smooth, around 2-3 minutes.

2. Add sugar to the milk and yogurt mixture. Blend until the sugar dissolves and you see a nice frothy layer.

3. Add cardamom, rose water and saffron strands (optional), and mix again.

4. Pour into a tall glass over ice. Garnish with chopped almonds or pistachios. You can also add a thick layer of fresh yogurt or cream on top for a decadent topping.

2 servings · 10 min · 10 min · blender or hand blender

kokum sharbat

Kokum Fruit Drink
by Indu Sona Mane

The kokum fruit (garcinia indica) native to Maharashtra, is the basis for this cooling drink, and can be found in Indian markets. Kokum is considered by practitioners of Indian Ayurvedic healers to have a wide array of medicinal and cooling properties. It is an anti-oxidant, skin-soothing and stomach-relieving coolant. The taste is mildly sour, and the fruit is also used in many Maharashtrian curries. The bright red juice makes for a beautiful, refreshing drink with a distinct flavor.

Ingredients

½ cup/ 120 ml dried or fresh chopped kokum

1 tsp/ 5 ml ground cumin

2 cups/ 475 ml sugar

Method

1. If you are using dried fruit, soak in hot water until soft for approximately 2 hours. Drain the water and continue to the next step.

If you are using fresh fruit, rinse the fruit, chop, and deseed but keep the outer skin.

2. Using a blender, puree fruit with cumin. Strain the puree discarding the solids.

3. Make a sugar syrup by boiling 1 cup of water with the sugar in a small pot. Mix well and the process should take around 10-15 minutes. Remove from heat to cool.

4. Mix together the strained puree and the cooled syrup which is a concentrate for the drink.

5. Add one fourth of the mixture to a large glass of cold water and mix well.

Garnish with black pepper, cardamom and salt. Serve chilled with ice.

4 servings | 20 min | 10 min | 2 hours (if using dried fruit) | blender

limbu sharbat

Sweet Lemon Juice
by Sangita Raut

This sweet-spicy chai-lemonade mixes surprising flavors for a distinctly Indian flavored lemon-mint refresher, great for hot days.

Ingredients

2-3 **medium** lemons

½ cup/ 120 ml hot water

1 tsp/ 5 ml chai masala

2 tsp/ 10 ml sugar

1 tsp/ 5 ml cumin powder

pinch of rock salt

few ice cubes

few mint leaves and lemon slices for garnish

Method

1. Squeeze the juice from the lemons into a cup and discard the seeds. Set aside.

2. To prepare the concentrate for this drink, pour ½ cup of hot water over chai masala and sugar into a mug and stir until the flakes are all melted. Add cumin and salt and stir well. Then add the lemon juice and stir again.

3. Pour the concentrate equally into 3-4 glasses. Add water and ice, and garnish with fresh mint leaves and lemon slices.

Serve chilled.

3-4 servings   10 min

jal jeera

Cumin Water
by Ragini Godbole

This drink, with a distinct cumin-mint flavor, is probably an acquired taste for most westerners. It is cool and refreshing but just a tad sour from the tamarind juice. It is often served at the beginning of a meal or in between courses, to cool the palate and aid in digestion.

Ingredients

- **2 tsp/ 10 ml** cumin seeds
- **1 tsp/ 5 ml** fennel seeds
- **1 Tbsp/ 15 ml** tamarind juice
- **¾ cup/ 177 ml** mint leaves, finely chopped
- **½ tsp/ 2.5 ml** black pepper
- **½ tsp/ 2.5 ml** amchur (dry mango powder)
- **pinch** of hing
- salt
- **1-2 cups/ 240-480 ml** soda water

Method

1. Dry roast the cumin seeds and fennel seeds in a small frying pan for 3-4 minutes until they are browned and aromatic.

2. In a blender, combine the roasted seeds with all the other ingredients and half a cup of water. Blend until the mixture is well combined.

3. Serve chilled by pouring the liquid into two glasses over ice, and topping up with soda water.

Serve chilled.

Manisha Sable

Manisha is from a town called Satara near the Krishna river in Maharashtra. Sangita and Manisha are best friends. They live next door to each other in Mumbai and their husbands work together in the same hotel. But Manisha and Sangita did not know each other before they moved to Mumbai. They became friends in Kalwa.

Manisha is unusual in that she has only one child, a son who is 17. She and her husband made the decision to have only one child in order to be able to provide for him economically in a substantial way. Manisha wears simple saris for work but has special golden embroidered saris for weddings and festivals.

Manisha shared that she stopped going to school when she got her period and that this is still upsetting to her.

Arriving in Mumbai ten years ago, Manisha and her husband moved because there were no schools where she grew up. Manisha is proud that her son is attending college.

In reflecting on the changes over the past ten years since moving to Mumbai, she explains that her husband now works in a jewelry factory. In addition to working in the collective, Manisha is one of the few women in the cooperative who holds another job as a cook for wealthy Mumbai families. Manisha learned how to cook from her grandmother because her mother was out working in the fields with Manisha's father. She fondly recalls that her grandmother taught her special techniques for stuffing puran poli and making sweet flatbreads, recipes that Manisha contributed to this cookbook.

The work in the collective is very important to Manisha. "Looking at the children and giving them food is very nice," she says. "It feels so good to give them food that we made. Seeing the smiles on their faces makes it all worth it."

She loves the village the most, because even after you sweat it out in the fields, it is still cooler there. It is healthier in the village.

"Being with the women, you get to know them and get to know other things, too," she says. "You learn new foods and new techniques." She is very happy being with them and cooking with them. She has new opportunities to learn from the women and be with them.

sol kadi

Coconut-Kokum Drink
by Manisha Sable

This cool drink uses pods of the Maharashtrian kokum fruit (garcinia indica) which can be purchased in an Indian market, to create an unusually spicy but cooling drink. This drink is very popular with Malvan cuisine and is often used as an appetizer or an accompaniment to a Thali meal, especially with fish curry and rice.

Ingredients

- **10-15** dried kokum pods
- **1 cup/ 240 ml** fresh coconut, grated, or **1 cup** of coconut liquid
- **1 small** green chili, finely minced
- **1-2 cloves** garlic, minced
- **2 tsp/ 10 ml** coriander powder
- **1 tsp/ 5 ml** cumin powder
- **½ tsp/ 2.5 ml** salt
- **few** mint leaves for garnish

Method

1. Soak kokum pods in 2 cups of warm water for 30-45 minutes.

2. Squeeze pods to extract juice. Discard the fruit and keep the juice. Set aside.

3. If you are using fresh coconut instead of coconut liquid, the steps for turning into a milk are as follows: Place it in a blender or food processor with 1 cup of water, until it forms a paste. Then place a strainer into a bowl with a cheesecloth over it. Pour the coconut mixture into the cheese cloth, then wrap the cloth around it and squeeze hard letting all the liquid drip into the bowl; this is your coconut liquid.

4. In a big bowl, mix the coconut liquid and the kokum liquid. Add all the spices and stir well. Or you may wish to put it back into the blender for a frothier beverage.

Garnish with mint leaves and serve chilled.

drinks

4 servings   15-20 min   ½ hour soaking   cheesecloth, strainer, blender

faluda

Milkshake

Our drink section would not be complete without Faluda, the sweet pink milkshake-like drink that is beloved by so many Maharashtrians, especially on a hot day. The primary ingredient, sabja, or basil seeds, can be found in most Indian shops, and it is well worth becoming familiar with. This super-seed is believed in both Indian and Chinese medicines to be useful with treating diabetes, hair loss, constipation, and excess weight and other issues. Many people take sabja every day by mixing it with a glass of water or warm milk, letting it soak for 5-10 minutes, and then drinking it. You can purchase all the ingredients as a pre-packaged mixture in Indian shops, for a sweet treat. Serve topped with a scoop of your favorite ice cream.

Ingredients

1 cup/ 240 ml milk

1 cup/ 240 ml rose water or regular water

½ cup/ 120 ml of Faluda Sev mix

2 Tbsp/ 30 ml sabja

scoop of ice cream for garnish

Method

1. Pour the milk and water into a medium sized saucepan and bring to a boil.

2. Lower the heat and add the faluda mix along with the sabja seeds and sev noodles. (Some mixes come with the sabja in the package.) The sabja softens and expands, then gets absorbed into the drink. Simmer on a low heat for 15-20 minutes, stirring occasionally.

3. When the mixture is foamy and well-blended, pour it into a pitcher and place it into the refrigerator for 4-6 hours or more to cool.

4. To serve, pour Faluda over ice and add a scoop of ice cream on top. Delicious!

2 servings   10 min   blender

The women prepare a variety of flavorful flatbreads – all on the stovetop. Many of the recipes here are prepared using a tawa, or griddle. Only one recipe in this section uses an oven – pav rolls, which are a Mumbai favorite.

breads

Classic Poori

Naan

Methi Poori

Moshe's Jeera Poori

Tikhat Bakri

Pav

Tikhat Poori

fasting

Westerners visiting India may get a strange shock if they see signs on restaurants that announce, "Fasting foods." There are special foods that people eat while they are "fasting". In other religious cultures, fasting generally means not eating any foods. But in Hinduism, the rules for fasting are not that way.

"Navrati" are nine-day sprints of fasting and worship that are celebrated across India. They are considered periods for serving the gods, as well as cleansing one's soul from wrongdoings that will cause suffering. It is an act of resolve that is meant to build character. Women only fast after they are married.

The "upvas", "vrats" – that is, the fasts – are observed by many people. This includes conducting a special "pujah" ritual in the morning and at night, avoiding wearing black, avoiding hair-cutting and shaving, and eating only one main meal a day (although it is permitted to eat light snacks during the day, such as fruit or nuts). There are also special chants that people recite before and after the meal, and there is a special "prasad" or food offering, to go along with it. Some of these customs differ between households. In addition, some of the women fast on other days during the year, some even once or twice a week. The women carry around upvas, special permitted foods, so that they are never too hungry.

foods

The foods that are forbidden are:
- Onions
- Garlic
- Heavy grains: wheat, chickpeas, soy
- Legumes
- Regular salt
- Common spices: turmeric, hing, garam masala, coriander, mustard

The foods that are allowed are:
- Light flours: buckwheat, amaranth, millet, and tapioca
- All fruits and vegetables
- All milk products
- Dry fruit
- Herbs: rock salt, coconut, sugar, honey, jaggery, cardamom, cloves, peppercorns, nutmeg, cinnamon, green chili, neem, curry, and ginger

classic poori

Round Crispbread
by Ranjana Ramchandra Gaikwad

This puffed-up, deep-fried, wheat-based, crispy flatbread can be a snack or the center of any meal. It goes well with curries, chutneys, and bhajis.

Ingredients

2 cups/ ½ liter white flour or atta (whole wheat flour)

3 Tbsp/ 45 ml rawa (semolina)

1 tsp/ 5 ml oil

1 tsp/ 5 ml salt

2/3 cup/ 160 ml water, room temperature

neutral oil for deep frying (e.g., sunflower, corn or canola)

Method

1. In a large mixing bowl, combine flour, rawa, oil, and salt. Gradually add water while kneading and knead well to form a dough. The dough should be smooth and firm – not sticky.

2. Divide the dough into small balls. You should have enough for around 10-12 pieces. Roll them out into flat, thin, round circles.

3. Heat oil in a deep-frying pan, wok, or kadai. When the oil is hot, add one poori at a time. Fry gently, pressing down with the slotted spoon in a circular motion. When the poori puffs up, after around 3-4 minutes, turn it to the other side and fry until it turns golden brown.

Serve the pooris hot with vegetable curries or gravies, or with sweet dishes like halwas.

TIP: Getting the pooris to come out as perfect circles is trickier than it looks. It helps to use a belan, a small rolling pin, which is easier to manipulate than the large, heavy ones. Also, the women of the collective hold the belan on the edges of the pin and not in the center. This technique helps spread the poori evenly. Finally, take your time. The women of the collective may spend 5-10 minutes on each poori getting it perfectly even, smooth and round.

10-12 pooris   10 min   30 min

 naan

Flatbread

This warm, soft, chewy flatbread, similar to Middle Eastern lafa, is made of refined wheat flour that is typically eaten with a wide variety of main dishes. It is great for dipping, sponging, and swiping, so to speak.

Ingredients

- **1 Tbsp/ 15 ml** sugar
- **2 tsp/ 10 ml** active dry yeast
- **1 ½ cups/ 360 ml** warm water
- **3 cups/ 381 gr** flour
- **1 tsp/ 5 ml** salt
- **1 tsp/ 5 ml** neutral oil (e.g., sunflower, canola or soybean)

Method

1. In a small mixing bowl, combine sugar and yeast with water that is warm but not hot. If the water is too hot, it will kill the yeast. Let it stand for 10 minutes until it gets foamy. At the end of the resting period, the mixture should be bubbly. If it is not, then the yeast did not ferment, and you need to start again.

2. In a large mixing bowl or an electric mixer with the dough hook, combine the flour and salt. Then pour in the yeast mix. Knead thoroughly for 5-10 minutes. When the dough is firm and not sticky, transfer it to an oiled bowl, cover with a damp cloth, and set aside for 30-40 minutes.

3. Place the dough on a floured workspace. Divide the dough into golf ball-sized balls. This recipe will make approximately 8-10 pieces. Roll out with a rolling pin or belan, into discs around ¼ inch or ½ centimeter thick.

4. Heat a tawa or frying pan. Add a little oil to keep from sticking. Place a flat dough onto the tawa and cook until it had brown spots, around 2-3 minutes, and then flip to the other side and do the same.

Serve this naan with any chutney, pickle, curry, or dip. Or wrap it like a tortilla, filled with your favorite sandwich bits.

TIP: You can add a variety of ingredients to the dough to create different flavored naans. Popular options include: garlic, chili peppers, basil, coriander, parsley, mint leaves, sundried tomatoes, or various combinations.

 8-10 naans   1 hour   20 min

breads

methi poori

Fenugreek Crispbread
by Indu Sona Mane

These savory crispy flatcakes made with fenugreek (methi) can be eaten hot, along with potato masala, chutney, or vegetables.

Ingredients

1 cup/ 240 ml whole wheat flour (atta)

1 cup/ 240 ml all-purpose white flour

3 tsp/ 15 ml rawa (semolina)

½ tsp/ 2.5 ml red chili powder

1 tsp/ 5 ml salt

½ tsp/ 2.5 ml jeera (cumin seeds)

½ cup/ 120 ml finely chopped methi (fenugreek leaves)

1 tsp/ 5 ml oil for the dough

½ cup/ 120 ml warm water

neutral oil for deep frying (e.g., vegetable, corn, or sunflower)

Method

1. In a large mixing bowl, combine the three flours. Add chili powder, salt, and cumin seeds and blend well. Finally add the fenugreek leaves and mix.

2. Add the oil, and then gradually add the water as you knead the dough, making sure there are no lumps. The dough should be smooth and firm – not sticky. Add more water if necessary. When the dough is soft, cover and set aside to rest for 30 minutes.

3. Form the dough into approximately 8-10 small pieces. Then using a belan or rolling pin, roll out the balls into discs approximately 3-4 inches or 8-9 centimeters in diameter.

4. In a wok or kadai, heat enough oil for deep frying. When the oil is sufficiently hot, place each disc into the oil and fry on each side, 2-3 minutes each, until they puff up and turn golden brown. Drain on a towel, paper towel, or in a colander.

Serve hot with potato masala, chutney, or your favorite vegetable.

10-12 rolls   40 min   20 min

moshe shek's jeera pooris

Cumin Seed Crispbread
by Chef Moshe Shek

The Masala Mamas traveled to Alibaug, Maharahstra, to the teaching kitchen of the famous Indian restauranteur, Moshe Shek. There, he taught the women some of his best secrets, including a recipe for his favorite pooris – jeera pooris made with "jeera" or cumin seeds. These are crispy flatbreads made with fenugreek seeds bringing a special flavor to this classic snack.

Ingredients

2 cups/ 256 gr white flour

1 tsp/ 5 ml neutral oil (e.g. sunflower or soybean)

1 tsp salt

½ cup/ 120 ml jeera (cumin seeds)

⅔ cup/ 160 ml milk

oil for deep frying

Method

1. In a large mixing bowl, combine flour, oil and salt. Add in the jeera seeds and mix again. Gradually add milk while kneading. Knead well to form a dough. The dough should not be soft but a little stiff and tight. Add water if necessary.

2. Divide the dough into golf ball-sized balls. You should have enough for around 12-14 balls. Roll them out into flat, thin, round circles.

3. Heat oil in a deep-frying pan, wok, or kadai. When the oil is hot, add one poori at a time. Fry gently, pressing down with the slotted spoon in a circular motion. When the poori puffs up, after around 3-4 minutes, turn it to the other side and fry until it turns golden brown.

Serve the pooris hot with curries or dips.

10-12 pooris   10 min   30 min

breads

a boatride to alibaug

Indian restauranteur Chef Moshe Shek opens his home and his heart to the Masala Mamas

Chef Moshe Shek, founder of the famous "Moshe's" cafe-restaurant chain in Awas, India, generously opened to the Masala Mamas his home and world-class kitchen from his culinary school, *A World Away*. He and his staff gave cooking lessons to the women, offering them some special tips from his dal, poori and other recipes, in order to help them improve their techniques by learning from one of the most successful chefs in the country.

The women – some of whom had never been on the water before – traveled by boat to Mr. Shek's retreat for the day and were treated to a lovely day of learning, eating, and relaxing in the beautiful country setting. Many of the women were so used to serving others that they had to get used to being served by Mr. Shek's staff.

"This was one of the best days we have ever had," said Indu. "It was a very special experience to be on the receiving end of Mr. Shek's incredible generosity."

Food takes on the energies of the people preparing it. Mr. Shek gave of his heart to support the women, just as the women give to the children with their hearts every single day. The Masala Mamas project is about food as a vehicle of love, and Mr. Shek embraced and modeled that energy as he supported the women.

tikhi bhakri

Spicy Wheat Flatbread
by Alka Harishchandra Gaikwad

This spicy bread uses a few different flours, including one called "jowar", or sorghum flour. This ingredient is being slowly discovered outside of India and is now considered to be the next superfood because of its many health benefits. It is gluten-free, high in protein and iron as well as other minerals, and is believed to control blood sugar. But be careful – this recipe uses raw chilis in the dough, so wear gloves even when you are kneading!

Ingredients

1 cup/ 128 gr besan (gram or chickpea flour)

1 cup/ 128 gr jowar flour (sorghum)

1 cup/ 128 gr wheat flour (atta)

1 onion, grated or finely diced

3-5 cloves garlic, crushed

1 Tbsp/ 15 ml cumin seeds

1 Tbsp/ 15 ml ajwain (carom) seeds

1 Tbsp/ 15 ml turmeric powder

2 green chili peppers, finely diced

1 tsp/ 5 ml salt

handful of coriander leaves

2 Tbsp/ 30 ml ghee or neutral oil (e.g., sunflower or canola)

¾ cup/ 177 ml warm water

Method

1. In a large mixing bowl, combine the three flours well. Add onion, garlic, cumin, ajwain, turmeric, green chili peppers, salt and coriander. Drizzle in the oil and then the water while kneading. Continue to knead until you have a stiff dough.

2. Divide the dough into roughly 10-12 golf ball-sized balls. Roll each one into a round disc, about ¼ inch thick. Each of these bhakri discs are ready to be fried.

3. Heat a skillet on medium-high heat and place each bhakri onto the skillet. When you see bubbles forming on the top side of the disc, after around 2-3 minutes, flip it to cook the other side. With a spatula, press on the top of the bhakri that has already been cooked. Turn it over and repeat, pressing it down. This makes the bhakri crispy. Once cooked on both sides, remove from the heat.

You can serve the bhakri with a dollop of ghee on top, or dipped in your favorite chutney. It is a tasty snack alongside chai.

10-12 bhakris

(option)

10 min

30 min

breads

pav
Rolls

These fluffy, western-style rolls can be eaten with vegetable stews or curries, fresh or toasted, topped with butter or ghee.

Ingredients

2 tsp/ 10 ml granulated dry yeast

2 tsp/ 10 ml sugar

2 Tbsp/ 30 ml oil

1 cup/ 240 ml warm water, divided

1 tsp/ 5 ml salt

3 cups/ 381 gr all-purpose flour (maida)

1 Tbsp/ 5 ml sugar and **¼ cup warm/ 60 ml** water for brushing

Method

1. In a large mixing bowl, combine yeast, sugar, oil, and ½ cup of warm water. The water should not be too hot or it will kill the yeast. Mix gently with a fork, then set aside for 10-15 minutes for the yeast to ferment. At the end of the resting period, the mixture should be bubbly. If it is not, then the yeast did not ferment and you need to start again.

2. When the yeast has fermented, add flour, salt and the rest of the water. Knead well. You can knead by hand or in an electric mixer using a dough hook. You want the dough to be firm and soft, but not sticky. Add more flour if necessary.

3. When the dough is ready, place it into an oiled bowl and cover with a moist towel. Let it rise for an hour. This is the first rise.

4. Once the dough has nearly doubled in size, it is ready to make the rolls. Oil a rounded or rectangular tin. Make fist-sized balls, roll them well in your hands to smooth them out and make them even in consistency, and then place them into the tin with a little bit of space in between. Note that the space between the rolls need not be too great because ideally you want the rolls to rise more and touch one another. Cover again with a damp cloth and let it rise a second time for 45 minutes. Meanwhile, preheat the oven to 180°C or 350°F.

5. Mix the sugar and water in a cup, and brush onto the rolls. Place in the oven uncovered for 20 minutes or until perfectly browned.

Serve the rolls with Pav Bhajji, fresh or toasted. You can also smear with ghee, or use the pavs for any sandwich of your choice. Or dunk them in your chai tea for a filling snack.

 10-12 rolls ½ hour   20 minutes 2 hours dough rising

breads

tikhat poori

Spicy Crispbread
by Jayshree Chavdry

This puffed-up, deep-fried, wheat-based, crispy flatbread can be a snack or the center of any meal. It goes well with curries, chutneys, and bhajis.

Ingredients

1 tsp/ 5 ml jeera (cumin seeds)

1 tsp/ 5 ml turmeric

4-5 cloves garlic, minced

3-4 green chili peppers, finely diced

1 cup/ 240 ml all-purpose white flour

1 cup/ 240 ml besan (gram flour or chickpea flour)

1 tsp/ 5 ml salt

½-¾ cup/ 120-180 ml of water

neutral oil for frying (e.g., sunflower, canola, or corn)

Method

1. In a large mixing bowl, combine the jeera, turmeric, garlic, chili peppers, flour, besan and salt. Gradually add ½ cup to ¾ cup of water as you knead into a dough. The dough should be smooth and firm.

2. Divide the dough into golf ball-sized balls – around 10-12 pieces. Using a belan rolling pin if you have one, flatten the pooris into discs.

3. In a deep-fryer, wok or kadai, heat oil for frying. Insert the discs, one at a time, and fry for 2-3 minutes on each side, until it puffs up and turns golden brown. Drain the pooris on a towel, paper towel, or in a colander.

Serve hot with your favorite curry, chutney, or pickle.

10-12 pooris   10 min   30 min

You won't find any cereal on the breakfast tables in Kalwa. The women prepare delicious, savory, hot meals very early in the morning – such as poha or upma – to make sure that their children go off to school with warm tummies.

breakfast foods

Aloo Paratha
Rice Dosas
Ghavan
Upma
Besan Dhirde
Sabudana Wada
Kanda Poha
Paneer Bhurji Paratha
Palak Paratha

festival foods,

Some of the women's most treasured cooking experiences revolve around festivals.

Sangita, for example, describes how Nag Panchami, a festival that celebrates the snake god, requires a food called Kanevle made of dal (lentils) and jaggery (sugarcane) batter that is cooked, boiled and then "fed" to the snake god along with milk.

The women also celebrate the Ganesh Chaturthi festival – a ten-day celebration during the Hindu month of Bhadrapada (usually August or September) that reveres the elephant-headed god Ganesha by offering him modaks. These labor-intensive yet delicious stuffed pastries – shaped like a cross between a chocolate kiss and a sun – are believed to be the favorite food of this god. During the festival pujah (ritual), he is presented with a prasad (platter offering) that should include 21 modaks. Once the god has received his modaks, everyone else can enjoy their own. Modaks can be steamed or fried, and can have a variety of fillings, including coconut, dried fruit, jaggery, or even dal.

For the popular Makar Sankranti festival that marks the sun's journey into the northern hemisphere, observed on January 14 every year, the women make a dish called Ambil that they offer in the Ram temple. It is made of jowar (sorghum flour) and turmeric, and has to be soaked in water for two days before the cooking begins.

This particular festival is also known for a unique Maharashtrian tradition of exchanging Tilgul Ladoo, special sweets made from sesame seeds and jaggery, as tokens of goodwill

while greeting each other with the words "*tilgul ghyaa, aani goad-goad bolaa*" meaning "Accept this tilgul (sweet) and utter sweet words". The gesture is meant to enter the year with feelings of goodwill while letting go of arguments and disagreements. We also used this greeting as the epigraph at the beginning of the book. It encapsulates so much of what the women transmit with food.

Hirabai says that during the month of Shrawan when there is a lot of fasting, the women have a special eating ritual. They sit down on the ground, and then throw a little water around the plate. They make a special blessing on the food – in particular, if someone has lost a family member. That moment is used to connect with their memory and exchange blessings with the departed. That is how they take the blessing of the food.

Sangita adds that the women regularly respect the fire god. After they prepare the food but before they eat it, they have to take out a bit from their plate and they keep it next to the fire or stove in order to please the fire god.

Indu also recalls making Faral, a collection of special sweets prepared for the festival of Diwali. When she was a child she learned how to make Faral – her aunts, sisters-in-law, cousins, and neighbors used to come together and prepare it. But now Indu has to make it all alone. Still, she always thinks about how much fun it was to make these sweets with all the women together, and longs for those days.

aloo paratha

Potato-Stuffed Flatbread
by Kalpana Gawde

This spicy potato-stuffed bread uses cloves and chili peppers to enhance the potato flavor. It can be eaten for any meal of the day including breakfast, or as a snack.

Ingredients

For dough:

2 cups/ 256 gr wheat flour

2 Tbsp/ 30 ml oil

¾-1 cup/ 180-240 ml warm water

½ tsp/ 2.5 ml salt

For filling:

2 Tbsp/ 30 ml oil

1 **medium** onion, diced

½ tsp/ 2.5 ml salt

2-3 **cloves** garlic, minced

2-3 **small** chili peppers, diced

3 **large** boiled potatoes, mashed

handful of coriander leaves, finely diced

ghee or oil for frying

Method

1. Prepare the dough. In a mixing bowl, mix together flour, oil, water and salt. Knead until the dough feels soft but firm, around 5-10 minutes. Cover with a damp cloth and set aside for 20 minutes.

2. Prepare the filling. Heat a frying pan and add oil. Add onions and salt, and sauté for 4-5 minutes until onions are soft and translucent. Add garlic and chili peppers and sauté for another 2-3 minutes. Add mashed potatoes and fry together for 4-5 minutes until potatoes have soaked in the spices. Add coriander and additional salt as needed. Remove from the heat and set aside.

3. Assemble the parathas by dividing the dough into 8 small balls/pieces. Roll each one out into a circle. Place a spoonful of stuffing at the center, and wrap up the dough around it so that you have a ball of dough around the stuffing. Seal the top with a drop of water. Roll out the dough once again into a circle with the potato mixture inside with the goal of creating a potato-stuffed thick pancake.

4. Heat the pan on a medium heat with one tablespoon of oil or ghee and fry the paratha for 5 minutes on each side until it begins to bubble and brown. Remove from the heat and serve with a dollop of ghee.

4 parathas | 30 min | 20 min

rice dosas

Rice-Flour Pancakes
by Maya Kadu

This soft, spongy, thin crepe batter prepared with rice flour, is delicious. However, it may be tricky to achieve exactly the right texture. The women of collective have practiced for years and prepare this staple with ease and grace. It is a delicious breakfast or snack.

Ingredients

2 cup/ 250 gr rice flour

3 cups/ ¾ liter water

1 tsp/ 5 gr salt

ghee or oil for frying (optional)

Method

1. Mix rice flour, water, and salt in a bowl until the pancake batter is lump-free and slightly liquidy.

2. Heat a tawa or non-stick frying pan over medium heat. Once the pan is hot, add a few drops of ghee or oil to keep the batter from sticking, although it often works best without oil.

3. Pour around ⅓ cup of batter into the pan and spread out into a round disc shape. The crepe should immediately start forming little bubbles. Cover the pan and let it cook for 2 minutes. Flip over and repeat on the other side. When both sides are spongy and bubbly, remove from heat. Repeat this process until you have a nice pile of soft dosas!

Serve hot, topped with butter or ghee, or your favorite breakfast topping.

breakfast foods

6-8 dosas

5 min

20 min

ghavan

Spicy Crepes
by Maya Kadu

These spicy crepes, a variation on rice dosas, are a Maharashtrian specialty.

Ingredients

2 cups/ 250 gr rice flour

½ tsp/ 1.25 ml salt

½ tsp/ 1.25 ml baking soda

3 cups/ ¾ liter water

1 green chili pepper, diced

1 tsp/ 5 ml cardamom powder

½ tsp/ 1.25 ml turmeric

1 Tbsp/ 15 ml neutral oil (optional)

Method

1. Mix together all the ingredients in a deep bowl, and whisk until it is a smooth batter with no lumps. Add more water if needed.

2. Heat a non-stick frying pan or tawa. You can use some oil to heat the pan if you'd like, but the recipe works well with no oil and the crepes turn out spongier. Pour a ladleful of the batter into the pan and spread it in a circular motion to make a flat crepe.

3. Cook on a medium flame for 1 to 2 minutes on each side. You can fry each crepe for a bit longer if you prefer a crisp crepe instead of a soft one. Repeat with the remaining batter.

Serve immediately with your favorite chutney or sambhar, flat or folded over.

 6-8 ghavans   10 min   15 min

Upma

Savory Porridge
by Indu Sona Mane

This semolina dish, filled with chilis, onions and spices, is considered a basic breakfast food. This is a simple, flavorful, and easy quick meal. Many people add different ingredients to make it more colorful, such as sautéed vegetables or dried fruit. You may also choose to add a bit of sugar to sweeten the taste either during the cooking process or when it is served.

Ingredients

- **1 cup/ 128 gr** semolina flour
- **1 Tbsp/ 15 ml** oil or ghee
- **¼ tsp/ 1.25 ml** mustard seeds
- **1 tsp/ 5 ml** dried red chilis
- **1 small** green chili pepper, diced
- **handful** of curry leaves, chopped
- **1 medium** onion, chopped
- **1 tsp/ 5 ml** salt
- **2 tsp sugar/ 10 ml** (optional)
- **2 ½ cups/ 580 ml** hot water
- coriander leaves for garnish

Method

1. Dry roast the semolina by putting into a completely dry saucepan over medium heat for 4-5 minutes, or until it is brown. Be careful not to let the semolina burn by continuing to mix it; the semolina should be brown on all sides. Set aside in a bowl.

2. In the same saucepan, heat oil on a medium flame. Add mustard seed, letting them "pop" which should take 1-2 minutes. Add the chili peppers and curry leaves and mix well. Then add the chopped onion and salt and stir so that the onion is well-coated with spices. Sauté for 3-4 minutes, or until the onions are soft.

3. Add the water and sugar (optional) to the roasted semolina and onion mixture and cook on a low flame, stirring with a wooden spoon. Cook until all the water is absorbed, around five minutes.

Garnish the upma with coriander and serve hot.

 2 servings (optional) 5 min 10 min

sangita raut

Sangita is not afraid of a little dough, or anything else, really. When it's time to make chapattis, she takes a big bowl of flour, water, and spices, pulls up her beautiful yellow and orange sari just a bit, then plants herself on the floor cross-legged and starts punching. With fire, energy, and some impressive biceps, she rolls and kneads, using unbridled strength and not even a tiny inclination that she is ready to let up. I watch her in awe as she spends half an hour whipping into shape a particularly feisty dough, laughing with her friend, Indu, and not getting even a drop of flour on her sari. This is a woman who knows how to get things done.

Sangita, a 39-year-old mother of four children – three girls and a boy. "Like me," I tell her, and Sangita gives me a sly, knowing smile. Coming from a large family in the village of Ahmednagar in Maharashtra about 120 kilometers north of Pune, Sangita's mother taught her how to cook. But when her husband got a secure job in the service industry, they moved to the Kalwa slum. Sangita was 15 years old, and had just gotten married to her husband, whom she met on the day she married him.

Sangita dropped out of school at the age of 12 because her family couldn't afford her education. She did not know anything about what to expect after she got married even though she had older married sisters – including one who got married and moved to Mumbai a few years before her.

Life in Kalwa is very different from life in the villages, but she admits that it is getting better. Recalling that there was no water and electricity, filth thrown on the streets, and no road to make walking to the nearby train station simple, they had to trudge into the city to get everything they needed, even the most basic supplies. But twenty years later, Sangita describes there being many more resources available in the slum including shops, vendors, and building – so daily life has gotten better. The place has also grown. In 2012, there were 120,000 people living in the Kalwa slum. Today, there are 200,000 – that's nearly double within five years.

Sangita's children are all in school with the oldest two in college. They are already more educated than she is, which makes her very happy. She says she would not be opposed to a marriage based on love – as opposed to an arranged marriage – an attitude that reflects some of the many changes that have taken place over one generation. Still, despite the educational opportunities that she has given her children by leaving her village to live in the city, she feels like she would go back to the village if she had the means. Her village is the place she truly loves.

Sangita loves to cook, and has been cooking since she was a girl. At first she would make her mother's recipes. But since then she has tried many dishes on her own, experimenting and trying to improvise; clearly the recipes have changed and that is something Sangita is proud of.

Sangita, is one of the managers, along with Indu, of the Delicio kitchen Masala Mamas cooperative. She has contributed some of her favorite recipes to the Masala Mamas cookbook: besan dhirde flatcakes, kanda lasun chutney made of garlic and onion, alu wadi rolls, and mattar paneer made of flavorful peas.

besan dhirde

Chickpea "Omelet"
by Sangita Raut

These crunchy, flavor-filled chickpea pancakes are a favorite Maharashtrian kid-friendly breakfast food. They also make a great omelet replacement for vegans. Dhirdes can be varied the same way you would make a traditional omelet by adding onion, tomatoes, or mushrooms into the batter. And for those who want a less spicy variation, you can replace coriander leaves with parsley leaves. This dish can be served with tomato sauce which is the way many Maharashtrian kids seem to prefer eating it for breakfast.

Ingredients

- **1 cup/ 128 gr** besan (chickpea flour)
- **2 Tbsp/ 30 ml** rava (semolina)
- **1 ½ cups/ 360 ml** warm water
- **1 Tbsp/ 15 ml** green chili paste or **1** small green chili, diced
- **1 Tbsp/ 15 ml** ginger-garlic paste
- **2-3 Tbsp/ 30-45 ml** chopped coriander
- **½ tsp/ 1.25 ml** turmeric
- **½ tsp/ 1.25 ml** hing
- **½ tsp/ 1.25 ml** jeera (cumin seeds)
- **pinch** of salt
- **1 tsp/ 5 ml** oil or ghee for frying

Method

1. Mix flours in a large bowl with warm water. Batter should be thick but liquidy enough to pour. Add chili paste, garlic paste, coriander, turmeric, hing, jeera and salt.

2. In a non-stick tawa or frying pan, heat a teaspoon of oil – not more or the dirdhi will be too oily. Pour a ladle-full of batter into the frying pan, and spread evenly into a round pancake shape. Cover with a lid and cook for 2 minutes.

3. Flip to the other side and cook again for 2 minutes and remove from heat.

Serve with coconut chutney or tomato sauce, although these are delicious on their own.

 6-8 dirdhis

 5 min
 15-20 min

breakfast foods

Sabudana Wada

Tapioca Fritters
by Sangita Raut

Tapioca is a popular base for certain foods because it is upvas – that is, it is allowed to be eaten during "fasts". Tapioca has little in the way of nutritional value or distinct flavor, but it is adaptable and filling, absorbing the tastes of what it is made with. It is also sticky, which makes it a good binding ingredient but can also be difficult to work with. Be sure to soak the tapioca pearls thoroughly until they are easily mashed between your fingers. Unsoaked tapioca has a tendency to "burst". These fritters are a common breakfast food. You can adjust the spices and other ingredients according to your tastes.

Ingredients

1 cup/ 240 ml tapioca pearls (subadana)

3 medium potatoes, boiled

½ cup/ 120 ml crushed peanuts or cashews

1 medium chili pepper, diced

1 chopped onion (if not intended for fasters)

¼ cup/ 60 ml diced coriander leaves

½ tsp/ 1.25 ml jeera (cumin seeds)

1 tsp/ 5 ml lemon juice

1 tsp/ 5 ml salt (or rock salt if intended for fasting)

neutral oil or ghee for frying

Method

1. Soak the tapioca pearls in water for 3-4 hours until they are easily mashed between your fingers. Drain and place in a large mixing bowl.

2. Mash the tapioca along with the potatoes. Add the nuts, chili pepper, onion, coriander, cumin, lemon juice, and salt and mix well into a smooth, firm batter.

3. In a large frying pan, heat a generous amount of oil. Make patties out of the batter, around the size of your palm, and place in the hot oil. Make sure the patties do not touch each other, since the tapioca has a tendency to stick. Fry until crispy brown, around 5 minutes, and then flip and fry on the other side. Remove from the oil when it is brown and crispy all around. Drain on a towel, paper towel, or in a colander.

Serve with chutney or ketchup.

breakfast foods

15-20 fritters | peanuts or cashews | 10 min | 30 min | 3-4 hours

breakfast foods

kanda poha

Riceflake Cereal with Onion
by Rohini Mahamuni

Poha, or pressed rice flakes, is a light, healthy breakfast favorite. Poha can be found in any Indian shop. Here, the recipe calls for mixing the poha with a colorful and flavorful combination of onions and vegetables. You can use pretty much any combination that suits you, including different vegetables, dried fruit, or nuts. It can be eaten hot or packed cold for picnics, lunches, or as a snack.

Ingredients

For the poha:

3 cups/ 700 ml of poha (pressed rice flakes)

½ tsp/ 2.5 ml turmeric powder

½ tsp/ 2.5 ml sugar (optional)

pinch of salt

For the mix:

1 Tbsp/ 15 ml neutral oil for frying (e.g., soybean, canola, or sunflower)

½ tsp/ 2.5 ml mustard seeds

½ tsp/ 2.5 ml cumin seeds

1 large red onion, diced

1 tsp/ 5 ml salt

2 small green chili peppers, diced

½ tsp/ 2.5 ml hing

1 medium potato, cubed

2-3 carrots, cubed

½ cup/ 120 ml peas or green beans, diced

1 tsp/ 5 ml lemon juice

2 tsp/ 10 ml grated coconut or parsley or coriander leaves for garnish

Method

1. Prepare the poha by rinsing the poha in a colander until it is moist but not drenched. Drain excess water, and then toss with turmeric, sugar, and salt. Set aside.

2. To prepare the mix, heat oil in a pan over medium heat. Add mustard and cumin seeds, and wait for the mustard seeds to "pop".

3. Add onion, salt, chili peppers and hing to the spiced oil, and sauté until golden brown.

4. Add potato, carrots, and peas or green beans and mix thoroughly. Cover, and allow to cook on a low heat until the potatoes are soft, around 15-20 minutes.

5. When the vegetables are soft, add the poha and mix thoroughly. Mix for five minutes until the flavors are well dissolved in the poha. Add lemon juice, and garnish with coconut.

Serve hot, or pack as a savory lunch.

breakfast foods

 4 servings   5 min 20 min

breakfast foods

paneer bhurji paratha

Cheese-Stuffed Flatbread
by Mangal Vittal Mane

This soft flatbread stuffed with a paneer mixture is one of many variations of the paratha. It can be made with a wide variety of stuffings other than cheeses, and is traditionally served with chutneys and sauces.

breakfast foods

Ingredients

For dough:

2 cups/ 256 gr wheat flour

2 Tbsp/ 30 ml oil

¾-1 cup/ 180-240 ml warm water

½ tsp/ 2.5 ml salt

For stuffing:

2-3 Tbsp/ 30-45 ml oil for sautéing vegetables

1 medium onion, finely chopped

½ tsp/ 2.5 ml salt

2-3 medium tomatoes, finely chopped

1 tsp/ 5 ml ginger-garlic paste

½ tsp/ 2.5 ml turmeric powder

1 tsp/ 5 ml red chili powder

1 tsp/ 5 ml garam masala

3.5 ounces/ 100 gr paneer

coriander leaves

2-3 Tbsp/ 30-45 ml of ghee or oil for frying parathas

Method

1. Prepare paratha dough. In a mixing bowl, knead together flour, oil, water, and salt, until the dough feels soft but firm, around 5-10 minutes. Cover with a wet cloth and set aside for 20 minutes.

2. Prepare stuffing. Heat oil in pan. Add in onions and salt and sauté until onions are light brown, around 4-5 minutes. Add tomatoes and continue to sauté for 4-5 minutes, until tomatoes are soft. Add ginger-garlic paste, turmeric, chili powder, garam masala, and sauté for another 2-3 minutes. Finally, add paneer (cheese) and sauté for two minutes. Add coriander, turn off the heat, and set aside.

3. Assemble the stuffed parathas. Divide the dough into golf ball-sized balls, around 2 inches or 4-5 cm in diameter. Roll out a ball into a circle trying to keep the dough thick, but not too thick. Add a spoonful of stuffing to the center of the pancake. Pull up the sides of the paratha to cover the stuffing, and pinch at the top with a bit of water. Roll out the stuffed paratha again into a flat pancake.

4. Heat up a frying pan and add one tbsp of oil or ghee for frying. Fry each paratha for 5 minutes on each side until they bubble up on the sides and turn brown.

Serve warm with your favorite chutney or dipping sauce.

 4 parathas   30 min   20 min

breakfast foods

palak paratha

Spinach-Stuffed Flatbread
by Kamal Shivaji Kadam

This spinach version of the classic unleavened flatbread "paratha" is a great way to incorporate spinach into a meal.

Ingredients

- 1 cup/ 240 ml diced spinach
- 1 cup/ 240 ml boiling water
- 1 tsp/ 5 ml ginger-garlic paste
- ½ cup/ 120 ml room temperature water
- 1 cup/ 128 gr wheat flour
- 1 cup/ 128 gr besan (gram or chickpea flour)
- 1 cup/ 128 gr of jowar (sorghum flour)
- 1 tsp/ 5 ml baking soda
- ½ tsp/ 2.5 ml salt
- ½ tsp/ 2.5 ml hing
- 1 tsp/ 5 ml ground coriander
- 1 tsp/ 5 ml ground cumin
- 2-3 Tbsp/ 30-45 ml oil for frying

Method

1. Blanch the spinach by pouring boiling over it in a saucepan, and letting it sit for 2-3 minutes – just to get it to wilt without losing its color. Drain the spinach and place the cooked spinach into a blender or food processor along with the ginger-garlic paste and ½ cup of water. Blend well. Let it cool for a few minutes so you will be able to touch it during kneading.

2. In a bowl combine the flours, baking soda, salt, hing, coriander, and cumin. Add the spinach when it has cooled and knead together. The dough should be firm and not sticky. Add more water or more flour to adjust the texture if needed.

3. Roll out the dough into golf ball-sized pieces. Then, using a belan or rolling pin, roll out each ball into a flat disc.

4. In a frying pan or tawa, heat 1 tsp of oil for each paratha. When the oil is hot, place a paratha into the pan. The dough should begin to form bubbles. After around 2-3 minutes when the paratha is brown around the edges, flip the paratha and cook for another 2-3 minutes. Remove from heat.

Serve warm with tomato sauce or chutney.

6-8 parathas   15 min   20-25 min   blender

breakfast foods

Indian food is known all around the world for its masalas, curries and chutneys. The women use a wide variety of local ingredients for sweet and savory dips – mangoes, coconuts, tomatoes, or paneer. Dips are a staple of every meal.

dips

Tomato Chutney
Curd Kadhi
Coconut Chutney
Mango Chutney
Muramba Kairicha
Kanda Lasun Chutney
Paneer Masala
Kala Chana Amti
Mango Pickle
Raita

Food is more than just for eating. Among the women of the collective, certain foods have other purposes as well, such as for cosmetics, for ritual purposes, and for healing.

One of the most important and versatile ingredients is turmeric, or haldi. It is considered especially vital for skin. Before weddings, brides are bathed in a turmeric-based mixture. Turmeric has special properties that clear the skin. Turmeric is also made into a paste that is used for a skin mask.

Turmeric also has ritual purposes. With its striking orange-rust color, it is one of the powders that is used for the bindis that women place on their foreheads.

Turmeric also has medicinal purposes. It is mixed with milk and given to children to heal colds, for example.

Another crucial ingredient is coconut oil, which is especially useful for healthy hair. The women share memories of sitting for weekly coconut oil treatments from their mothers. This entails rubbing oil over clean hair and then designing a tight braided hairstyle. Girls are expected to keep this hairstyle for a week so the oil can stay in the hair. Indeed, the women all have thick, shiny hair, and credit the coconut oil treatment of their youth. Today, many women report that their daughters prefer to get their hair done in salons rather than with their mothers' coconut oil treatment. But Hayley, for example, still does the coconut oil treatment for her daughter every week.

Rice water, which is the water left over after parboiling rice, is also considered healthy for hair. Some women rinse their hair with the water, like a conditioning treatment.

Some of the ingredients are still unknown outside of Maharashtra. A spice called owha is considered especially good for healing colds. The spice is dry-roasted in a pan and then inhaled like vapor. It is even given to babies, and put it in the ears of the baby to clear ear infections.

The women report that they had much more knowledge of how spices were used for healing and cosmetics when they lived in their villages. Today, in the city, that knowledge is no longer valued, and is no longer preserved. This is just one more cultural artifact that has been lost with the women's migration to the city.

tomato chutney

Tomato Dip
by Kalpana Gawde

The array of spices brings out the tomato flavor in this classic chutney. This can also be made as a raw tomato chutney, using hard, unripened green tomatoes and eliminating the onion. Note that this recipe uses lentils as a spice. The urad dal (yellow split pea) gets dry roasted in the pan along with the seeds. This chutney can be eaten with almost anything – samosas, pooris, or any savory snack.

Ingredients

- **1 Tbsp/ 15 ml** urad dal (black gram lentils)
- **1 Tbsp/ 15 ml** sesame seeds
- **2 Tbsp/ 30 ml** oil
- **1 tsp/ 5 ml** cumin seed
- **2 small** green chili peppers, diced
- **1 medium** onion, diced
- **½ tsp/ 2.5 ml** of salt
- **¼ tsp/ 1.25 ml** tsp hing
- **½ tsp/ 2.5 ml** turmeric
- **1 Tbsp** garlic-ginger paste
- **1 cup** plum or beefsteak tomatoes, de-seeded and diced
- **2 Tbsp/ 30 ml** sugar
- **1 Tbsp/ 15 ml** tamarind juice
- salt to taste

Method

1. Dry roast the urad dal and sesame seeds in a frying pan on a low flame with no oil for approximately 4-5 minutes or until golden brown. Cool and set aside.

2. In a pan, heat oil, cumin, and chili peppers on a medium flame. Add diced onion and salt and cook until onions are translucent, around 5-7 minutes. Add hing, turmeric, and garlic-ginger paste and stir for another 2-3 minutes.

3. Add tomatoes and continue to cook until tomatoes become soft. When tomatoes are nearly soft, add the sugar and tamarind and cook for another 5 minutes.

4. Now grind the dal using your choice of method – spice grinder, mortar and pestle, etc. (see introduction) and add to the frying pan. Continue cooking for another 4-5 minutes until the chutney is soft. Add more salt to taste.

5. The chutney can be blended for a pureed texture, or left chunky. It can be served cold or hot and goes well with chapattis, pooris, breads, rice, and a wide variety of savory dishes.

 6-8 servings   sesame 10 min 20 min

dips

curd kadhi

Yogurt Stew
by Alka Harishchandra Gaikwad

A warm and savory yogurt-based sauce that is easy, creamy, and perfect over rice, this recipe varies by region in India. This Maharashtrian version is sometimes a bit sweeter than others, and you have the option of adding a teaspoon of sugar with the spices for a sweeter base. This is a great recipe for an easy summer supper, or, you can serve with pakoras or, as a soup.

Ingredients

1 cup/ 240 ml plain yogurt ("curd")

1 tsp/ 5 ml besam (gram flour)

1 cup/ 240 ml of water

2 tsp/ 10 ml ghee or any neutral oil (e.g., canola, sunflower, or vegetable)

1 tsp/ 5 ml mustard seeds

1 tsp/ 5 ml cumin seeds

1 tsp/ 5 ml ginger-garlic paste or **½ tsp/ 2.5 ml** grated ginger and **½ tsp/ 2.5 ml** minced garlic

2 small green chili peppers, diced

handful of curry leaves, finely chopped

handful of coriander leaves finely chopped

1 tsp/ 5 ml turmeric powder

1 tsp/ 5 ml salt

1 tsp/ 5 ml sugar (optional)

Method

1. Place the yogurt into a mixing bowl with the besam and whisk gently. Add water, up to a cup, and continue whisking – either by hand or with a hand blender – until no lumps remain.

2. Heat a medium-sized saucepan. Pour in the oil or ghee and heat. Add mustard seeds and cumin seeds and heat until the mustard seeds "pop". Then add ginger-garlic paste and chopped green chili peppers. Sauté for a minute until the raw flavor from the garlic is gone.

3. Add curry leaves and coriander leaves; sauté for a minute.

4. Pour the yogurt mixture into the pot over the spice mix. Bring to a boil. Add additional water if necessary to keep the mixture thick but liquidy.

5. Add turmeric powder and salt, and sugar if you wish, adjusting amounts if necessary to your taste. Mix well and let kadhi simmer for 7 minutes on a low flame.

Serve hot with steamed rice.

6 servings

10 min

10 min

dips

alka harishchandra gaikwad

Alka, one of the elder women of the cooperative, is not sure how old she is. She got married at the age of 14, and has four children – two boys and two girls – but cannot even say exactly how old they are. Originally from the villages of Jharegaon and Karmala Takula in Solapur, Alka has been in Mumbai for probably forty years and guesses that she got married somewhere around the age of 12. Her children are now in their twenties and thirties.

Alka's life is the story of a woman who did not go to school. Yet, in this space of the women's cooperative, Alka is revered for her life wisdom attained not in a classroom but at home from her mother and the community of women around her. She learned to cook when she was very small just by being around her mother. She was never formally taught, but learned by observation, osmosis and later on experimentation. The women in the cooperative not only look up to Alka and seek her guidance, they also positively adore her.

Alka is originally from the villages of Jharegaon and Karmala Taluka near Solapur. She loves her village and goes back regularly for festivals and occasions like weddings where she gets to celebrate with her extended family. "People are usually very busy working the field," she explains, "so they relish the opportunity to come together."

Alka has land in her village where they grow many varieties of fruits like bora berries. Since they did not grow rice in her village, she has fond memories of wheat-based dishes, like the Puran Poli that is a favorite of so many women. The cooperative has become a place where recipes are shared and cultures are exchanged.

Alka has contributed some classic Maharashtrian favorites to the cookbook: Tikki Bhakri, Curd Kadhi, Maswadi, Egg Curry, and Balushahi.

"I love it over here." Alka shares with me comparing her life now as part of the collective to the years before it began. "I've always been alone, at home, and now I have the opportunity to do something – to show what I can do." She likes coming out to the group and "opening her mind and trying new things."

Alka has reached a stage in life when she is looking for something more. Her children are all working professionals, some are already married, and she is ready for new things to do. She hopes to set up a snack stand at the Gudi Padwa New Year's festival that Maharashtrian Hindus celebrate every spring. The work with the cooperative gave Alka the courage and the push to imagine more for herself, and I imagine that Alka's example will lead other women of the collective to do the same in the coming years.

coconut chutney

Coconut Dip
by Maya Kadu

This cooling and sweet Maharashtrian favorite goes well as a dip to many sweet and savory snacks.

Ingredients

1 cup/ 240 ml fresh flaked or grated coconut, or frozen

1 green chili pepper

½ tsp/ 2.5 ml salt

½ inch/ 2 cm ginger

1 clove garlic

½ tsp/ 2.5 ml powdered cumin

¼ cup/ 60 ml water

2 Tbsp/ 30 ml neutral oil (e.g., sunflower or canola oil)

½ tsp/ 2.5 ml mustard seeds

½ tsp/ 2.5 ml cumin seeds

¼ tsp/ 1.25 ml hing

8 curry leaves

5-6 cloves of garlic

Method

1. Place coconut, green chili pepper, salt, ginger, garlic, cumin, and water in a blender until you get a fine paste. Add a little more water if needed. Pour mixture into a bowl.

2. Take a small saucepan and heat the oil. When hot, add mustard and cumin seeds. Continue by adding hing and curry leaves. Pour the spiced oil over the coconut mixture. Mix well.

Serve with Idlis, Medu Vada, Masala Dosa, savory Appes, or with chapattis or rice.

4 servings | coconut | 6-7 min | 2-3 min

Mango Chutney

Mango Dip
by Kamal Kadam

A versatile favorite among the women of the collective, this chutney is cool, sweet and refreshing, and goes well with almost any meal. It can also be mixed with other dressings and sauces and used creatively in a variety of salads or other recipes that call for a sweet touch.

Ingredients

- **1 Tbsp/ 30 ml** neutral oil
- **2 tsp/ 10 ml** curry powder
- **½ tsp/ 2.5 ml** ground nutmeg
- **½ tsp/ 2.5 ml** ground cinnamon
- **1 Tbsp/ 15 ml** cayenne pepper
- **½ tsp/ 2.5 ml** salt
- **4 cloves** garlic, peeled and crushed
- **1 cup/ 240 ml** finely chopped onion
- **1 Tbsp** grated fresh root ginger
- **½ medium** sweet red pepper, chopped
- **2 medium** apples, peeled, cored and chopped
- **2 cups/ 400 gr** sugar
- **2 cups/ ½ liter** white wine vinegar
- **1 Tbsp/ 5 ml** lemon juice
- **3-4 large** mangoes, peeled, cored and sliced

Method

1. In a large saucepan, heat the oil. Add the curry, nutmeg, cinnamon, cayenne pepper and salt, and cook for 2-3 minutes until it becomes aromatic. Add garlic, onion, ginger and red pepper and sauté in the spice mixture for 3-5 minutes until soft.

2. Add the apples, sugar, vinegar and lemon juice, and cook over a low heat until the sugar is dissolved, around 5 minutes.

3. Add the chopped mangoes. Bring to a boil and then simmer for an hour until the chutney is thick and syrup-like.

4. Spoon into sterilized jars and seal.

The chutney can stay for a very long time, up to around two months. If they are properly canned using a canning technique and stored in a dark, cool place, it can keep for a year.

1-2 liters   15 min   1 hour   Jarring equipment for canning

dips

maya kadu

Maya, 32, is one of the youngest women in the cooperative. She, like her dear friend Alka who is one of the elders, has had very little schooling and sometimes struggles with ages and addition. Her two children are 16 and 12 years old, which suggests that she was married around the age of 15 or earlier. She and her husband left their village near Pune right after they got married because her husband got a job in Mumbai.

Maya talks fondly about Pune which is famous for fruits like anjeers and mangoes. Every year around mango season, typically in April or May, Maya goes back to Pune. They go for the fruit, but they stay for the family. "We are both from Pune," she says referring to her husband, "so we have double the family celebrations every time we go back."

Even though she misses her village and finds Mumbai to be very hot, the women's cooperative has brought Maya a lot of satisfaction in her life. "I love being with the women," she says "and coming together." Maya tells me that she especially likes being with elder women, like Alka, with whom she has a very close relationship.

Maya, like all the women, reminisces about the food in her village and about the experiences of cooking together. Pune is a rice-based agriculture – as opposed to the wheat-based systems in the villages of other women in the cooperative – so Maya favors rice dishes, like the vegetable biryani that she contributed to this cookbook. She also shared the recipes for ghavan, coconut chutney, muramba kairicha, potato bhaji and dudhi halwa, and tells me how much she enjoys vegetarian cooking.

muramba kairicha

Mango Preserve
By Maya Kadu

This sweet, aromatic preserve made of grated raw green mango, a favorite among Maharashtrian children and adults alike, is a specialty dish that many women make once a year during mango season. It requires special care and attention in the cooking process in order for the mango to retain its stringiness, so that it comes out as jam and not a syrup. The preserve can last for many months – the entire mango season – and is enjoyed as a dip with a variety of breads and snacks.

Ingredients

1 medium green (unripe) mango

1 tsp/ 5 ml ghee

¾ cups/ 177 ml chopped jaggery

½ tsp/ 2.5 ml cardamom powder

6 cloves

Method

1. Wash, peel, and grate the mangoes with a grater or in a food processor. You should have approximately one cup of fruit.

2. Heat ghee in a saucepan or kadai. Add jaggery and mix over a low flame. Stir until the jaggery melts, around 10-15 minutes.

3. Add grated mango. Sauté and cover for 2-3 minutes over low heat.

4. Add cardamom powder and cloves. Sauté and cover for ten minutes over low heat; do not over boil. The syrup thickens a bit more after cooling down.

5. Remove from heat, stir, and cool completely.

Transfer the muramba into a sterilized and completely dry glass jar. Serve muramba with chapatti, paratha, or bread.

yields 1-2 cups   coconut   10 min   30 min   blender or grinder

kanda lasun chutney

Onion-Garlic Spice Mix
by Sangita Raut

This aromatic spice mix with an onion-garlic base is more of a masala than a chutney. It is famous in Maharashtra and used in dishes ranging from meat and fish to beans and vegetables. (See the recipe for kala chana amti for an example of its use with beans.) True devotees spend hours, even days, perfecting the spice method, and will sometimes use some heavy equipment, like the "mirchi kandap" an elaborate contraption for grinding complex spice mixtures that some women swear by. The recipe presented here uses a very quick method for roasting spices and works well. Plus, if you've never tried roasting dry coconut flakes, this is a great opportunity to experience this wonderful practice. It will fill your kitchen with amazing aromas.

Ingredients

- **1 cup/ 240 ml** dry grated coconut flakes
- **1 Tbsp/ 15 ml** oil for frying
- **3 large** red onions, finely diced
- **1 tsp/ 5 ml** salt
- **½ cup/ 120 ml** sesame seeds
- **1 large** garlic, minced
- **¾ cup/ 177 ml** garam masala
- **1 cup/ 240 ml** red chili powder
- **½ cup/ 120 ml** oil for mixing

Method

1. Heat a frying pan and add coconut flakes. Dry roast them until they turn brown. Set aside.

2. Heat oil in a frying pan. Add the red onions and salt. Sauté onions on a low flame. Caramelize but do not burn – around 6-7 minutes. Set aside.

3. Grind the coconut with the garlic and sesame seeds, either electrically in a coffee grinder or by hand using a mortar and pestle or the "chef's method" of crushing in baking paper with a large chef's knife. Add the onion and continue to crush or grind the mixture.

4. When everything is ground to a powder, add the garam masala and chili powder and mix well.

5. Finally, add the oil to form a paste. The mix should be damp but not wet.

Store the mixture in an airtight container in the fridge. It can last for a very long time when properly sealed. This spice mix is great when you are looking for a strong flavoring in a main dish.

Makes 3 cups   10 min   10 min   Coffee grinder, mortar and pestle, or other spice grinding equipment

dips

paneer masala

White Cheese Stew
by Mangal Vittal Mane

This tomato-cheese dish blends the texture of the white-cheese paneer with the flavors of cashews, onions, tomatoes and Maharashtrian spices. The women make their own tomato paste out of seeded plum tomatoes or beefsteak tomatoes. But you can also substitute store-bought tomato paste for a quicker result. Also, this recipe calls for making your own cashew paste, used in many paneer recipes to add a creamy texture. The women of the collective consider cashew paste to be an important flavoring for all kinds of curries and chutneys. The cashews and tomato paste are a particularly popular flavor combination.

Ingredients

15 whole cashews

water for soaking cashews and **2 Tbsp/ 60 ml** warm water

3 large tomatoes

2-3 Tbsp/ 30-45 ml oil or ghee

1 Tbsp/ 15 ml ginger-garlic paste

2-3 bay leaves

1 large onion, grated

1 green chili pepper, diced

1 Tbsp/ 15 ml red chili powder

1 Tbsp/ 15 ml coriander powder

1 Tbsp/ 15 ml cumin powder

1 Tbsp/ 15 ml garam masala powder

½ cup/120 ml milk

½ cup/ 120 ml water

1 tsp/ 5 ml salt

8 ounces/ 250 gr paneer cut into 1-inch cubes

2 Tbsp/ 30 ml methi leaves (dry fenugreek leaves)

Method

1. First, prepare your cashew paste. Soak the cashews in warm water for 45 minutes. Grind the soaked cashew nuts with 2 tablespoons of warm water in a blender in order to make cashew paste.

2. Next prepare your tomato paste. Peel and deseed the tomatoes, then place them in a saucepan with boiling water, and boil for 4-5 minutes. Remove tomatoes from the water and blend in a blender, food processor, or grinder. Blend until you have the texture of a puree.

3. Heat cooking oil or ghee in a large saucepan over a medium flame. Add ginger-garlic paste and bay leaves, and sauté. Then add grated onion and sauté until onion turns light brown – approximately 4-5 minutes.

4. Add green chili pepper and red chili powder and sauté for a minute. Add cashew nut paste. Stir and cook for 2 minutes. Add tomato puree and cook until oil starts to separate from the puree, around 3-4 minutes.

5. Add coriander powder, cumin powder, and garam masala powder and mix well. Add milk, ½ cup water, and salt. Mix and cook on a low heat until oil comes to the surface, around 4-5 minutes.

6. Add paneer cubes and fenugreek leaves, and cook for approximately 2 minutes or until you get desired consistency of gravy.

Transfer prepared curry to a serving bowl. Garnish with coriander leaves, paneer, cream or a cube of butter and serve.

4-6 servings

cashews

15 min

25 min

45 min
soaking cashews

blender or grinder

dips

kala chana amti

Black Chickpea Stew
By Kalpana Gawde

When the women of the collective say "chickpeas" – "chana" – they usually mean split yellow chickpeas. When they want to refer to whole chickpeas, they usually call it "black chickpeas" or "kala chana", which are whole and brownish chickpeas. This black chickpea gets its reddish hue from the kanda lasun chutney a hot Maharashtrian spice mix. This dish is packed with flavor and goes well served with rice.

Ingredients

- 4 Tbsp/ 60 ml oil, divided
- 1 sliced onion
- 2 Tbsp/ 15 ml grated coconut
- 2 Tbsp/ 30 ml raw urad dal (yellow split lentils)
- 1 tsp/ 5 ml cumin seeds
- pinch of hing
- 2 bay leaves
- 3 minced garlic cloves
- 3 Tbsp/ 45 ml kanda lasun chutney
- ½ tsp/ 2.5 ml turmeric powder
- 1 tsp/ 5 ml salt
- 1 cup/ 240 ml chickpeas (soaked overnight)
- 1 Tbsp/ 15 ml tamarind juice
- chopped coriander leaves for garnish

Method

1. Heat oil in pan and sauté onions on a medium flame till golden brown. Add coconut, mix well, and then remove from heat and allow to cook without burning the coconut. When the coconut has browned, place the mixture into a blender or food processor along with the urad dal and half a cup of water. Grind to a paste.

2. In a medium saucepan, heat remaining oil on a medium heat. Add cumin seeds, hing, bay leaves and garlic and cook for 2-3 minutes. Add the ground onion paste, kanda lasun, turmeric and salt to taste. Lower the flame and cook for 3-4 minutes, stirring constantly so that it doesn't burn.

Add soaked chickpeas, 2 cups of water, and tamarind juice. Bring to a boil, and then cook covered on a very low heat for 45 minutes until chickpeas are tender.

Garnish with chopped coriander. Serve with rice or chapattis.

 4 servings   coconut, cashews, sesame seeds 15 min 45 min overnight soak and spice prep blender or grinder

dips

hayley dsouza

GPM Educational Program Director Hayley Dsouza

Hayley, a very beloved staff member who, among other things, coordinates the GPM school programs in Kalwa, has been working with GPM for nearly five years. She loves the children, and is motivated by the ability to make a difference in their lives.

"I don't consider this a job anymore," she says. "It is something I love to do. Seeing the smiles on the kids' faces brings me lots of joy."

Hayley has been invaluable to the Masala Mamas cookbook project. She served as unofficial translator and cultural interpreter for the women. Her coordination has been key in enabling us to turn the women's knowledge of food and culture into recipes that the world can learn about and appreciate. Most importantly, Hayley's love for the people she works with comes through in everything she does.

Hayley contributed two wonderful recipes to the cookbook: the delicious chili-mushroom pakoras, and her mother's mango pickle recipe, which may take three weeks to prepare, and brings back charming memories from her childhood. Hayley lives in Thane with her husband, Lloyd and ten-year-old daughter, Faith.

mango pickle
by Hayley Dsouza

This recipe holds a record: it is the dish that requires the longest preparation time in this cookbook – nearly three weeks! This delicacy comes from the mother of Hayley Dsouza, the Educational Coordinator of Gabriel Project Mumbai. Hayley describes how as a child, she and her brother were tasked with guarding the mango while it had to stay in the sun for up to 19 days. She admits that they may have snuck a few pieces along the way. This dish, like so many mango dips, is considered a once-a-year specialty, celebrating the beloved mangoes in season.

Ingredients

- **3 large** raw mangoes
- **1 cup/ 240 ml** mustard oil
- **2 ½ Tbsp/ 35 ml** fennel seeds
- **1 Tbsp/ 15 ml** fenugreek seeds
- **1 Tbsp/ 15 ml** salt
- **2 ½ tsp/ 12 ml** turmeric powder
- **2 tsp/ 10 ml** mustard seeds
- **2 Tbsp/ 30 ml** red chili powder
- **2 tsp/ 10 ml** black cumin (kalonji)

Method

1. Heat mustard oil in a non-stick pan till it starts to smoke. Set aside to cool.

2. Wash the mangoes, and then cut them into quarters, leaving the skin on. Next, remove the tender seeds and cut into smaller pieces and place in a large glass bowl.

3. Grind fennel seeds and fenugreek seeds using a coffee grinder, mortar and pestle, or other technique. Add salt, turmeric powder, mustard seeds, red chili powder, and black cumin to the crushed seeds and mix well. Pour over the cut mangoes.

4. When the oil is cooled, add half of it to the mango-spice mixture and blend well. Keep the bowl in the sun for 3-4 days. It is best to cover the glass bowl with a net or a cover to keep away insects and animals. Afterwards, transfer into a porcelain or glass jar and add the remaining oil so that all the mango pieces are well covered. Keep the jar tightly closed, and place it in the sun for an additional 12-15 days.

The mango pickle is ready to eat!

 yields 2 cups   20 min   5 min 19 days blender or grinder

raita

Yogurt Dip

This cooling dip is a must at Indian meals, to balance the digestive system after eating hot foods. The cucumber, cumin and dill all have balancing effects on the palate and stomach. And it also tastes delicious — perfect for dipping chili mushroom pakoras and other spicy delights.

Ingredients

1 cup/ 240 ml yogurt

1 medium cucumber, diced

1 tsp/ 5 ml cumin powder

1 handful of dill, diced

1 handful of coriander leaves, diced

1 small purple onion, finely diced (optional)

salt and pepper to taste

Method

Mix all the ingredients. Serve chilled. Garnish with dill or coriander leaves, or cucumber slices.

yields 1 cup 10 min

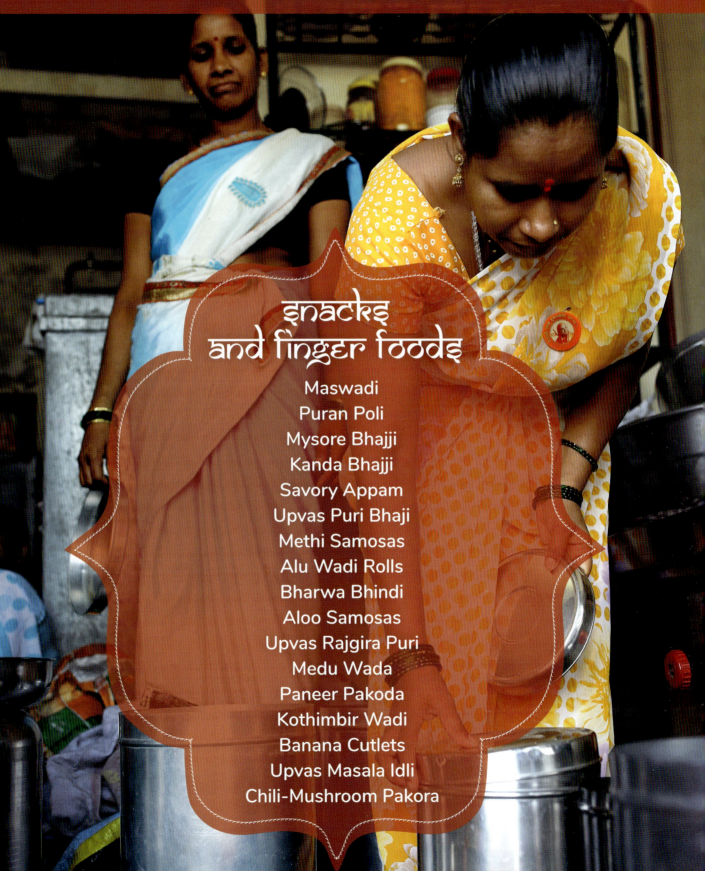

The women invest a lot of time and love into their sweet and savory snacks. The snacks have a variety of fillings, they can be eaten with tea or on their own, and they ensure that robust flavors fill the women's homes all day long.

snacks and finger foods

Maswadi
Puran Poli
Mysore Bhajji
Kanda Bhajji
Savory Appam
Upvas Puri Bhaji
Methi Samosas
Alu Wadi Rolls
Bharwa Bhindi
Aloo Samosas
Upvas Rajgira Puri
Medu Wada
Paneer Pakoda
Kothimbir Wadi
Banana Cutlets
Upvas Masala Idli
Chili-Mushroom Pakora

the evolution of the arranged marriage

The women of the collective have many things in common. They are all originally from Maharashtrian villages and now living in Kalwa. They are all married – except for Mangal whose husband recently died. They are all mothers. They all learned to cook in order to prepare for marriage. They all got married in their teens. They all left school to get married – some barely went to school at all. All their marriages were arranged marriages. All their husbands are 10-15 years older than them. And, none of them met their husbands until the wedding day.

The arranged marriage is a tradition that has belonged to many cultures around the world, since time immemorial. The *Bible* is filled with stories of arranged marriages – such as how Abraham sent his servant hundreds of miles away to find a suitable wife for his son, Isaac. But not all arranged marriages are the same.

When the women were growing up in their villages, marriage was a matter of word of mouth. One person would tell another in their village or district that they have someone who is ready for marriage, and they would exchange details and ideas. If things proceeded well, the parents would meet in each other's houses, meet the prospective spouse, check out the important issues – such as finances, religion, profession, horoscope, social standing – and then proceed. That is, the parents would proceed. The process could take months, even years. But the bride did not have a say in the matter.

"I don't know how I felt about the man," Hirabai said when asked about this. "We didn't talk about it." The women got married between the ages of 12 and 17, roughly, to men who are around ten years older than them. The girl is fully expected to move to her husband's family home, but she also changes her clothing and appearance. As a sign of being married, Maharashtrian women wear green bangles, mangalsutra (gold necklaces), red bindis on their foreheads, wedding rings on their toes and bell bracelets on their ankles. Before they get married, girls can wear jeans and modern clothes. But with marriage, gone are the jeans and they begin to wear only saris. Also, when visiting their husband's parents, daughters-in-law are expected to wear head coverings and greet the in-laws by falling at their feet as a sign of respect.

The only time a girl is allowed to stay with her own family instead of her husband's, Subhadra explained, is if there are no boys in her family. But then the pressure is on the man to take care of both families – his own and his wife's.

India boasts a very low divorce rate – some 2% – even with the majority of marriages being arranged. However, this might also reflect the fact that even women who might wish to leave their husbands often do not have the ability to express that. "Even if they didn't like the boy, they would marry him," Kamal said about the way marriages took place in her village.

"There was a girl from my village who didn't like the man," Kamal reflected. "She is still married to him, but it's not good. They are always fighting, and they are still stuck in the marriage because of the kids. There are women who are not happy, but divorce doesn't happen. Maybe one in a hundred."

Today, however, the arranged marriage looks a bit different. Certainly, the women all prefer their daughters to seek arranged marriages – as do an estimated 74% of Indians aged between 18-35 years according to a 2013 IPSOS study.[1] However, today an arranged marriage is not a forced marriage. Most of the women fully expect their daughters to approve of the boy, and definitely meet a few times before the wedding, unlike the way they themselves got married. "Girls won't get married today unless they have a say," Kamal explained. The marriage in which the couple does not meet until the wedding day is a thing of the past. "Everything is changing."

Another big change is that now some couples live on their own. In Kalwa especially, nuclear families live on their own, not with their extended families. Do the women like this? "Not at all! We would much prefer to live with in-laws and family," women told me in unison. "Even in regular life, even when there are disagreements, it is better to be with family."

And of course, the women's daughters are all completing their education. That is something that the women are very proud of. Most of the women would have liked to stay in school themselves.

When it comes to marriage and family life, things are changing – and the women are adapting in their own ways. "Our daughters will not have a love marriage," Subhadra said, referring to the idea of people simply meeting on their own and deciding to get married for love. "But who knows, maybe our granddaughters will."

"If my daughter came to me and said she wanted to marry for love," Sangita said, "I would consider it."

Change indeed.

---

1 Kavita Das, "India has changed a lot in 70 years. But arranged marriage remains the norm." Washington Post, May 2 2017 https://www.washingtonpost.com/news/soloish/wp/2017/05/02/india-has-changed-a-lot-in-70-years-but-arranged-marriage-remains-the-norm/?utm_term=.740c7c02f83a; "Indians swear by arranged marriages," India Today. March 4, 2013 http://indiatoday.intoday.in/story/indians-swear-by-arranged-marriages/1/252496.html

Besan Fritters

by Alka Harishchandra Gaikwad

This savory, spicy besan-based roll is one of the most favorite finger foods in Maharashtra. There are several intricate steps involved, some of which will probably sound strange to non-Indian cooks. The process involves steaming an entire roll on a greased steamer. We offer an alternative method here, in which the roll is sliced first and then steamed. We also experimented with pan-searing the pieces to add crispiness. Either way, the result is worth it. Special thanks to Chef Jay Engelmayer for his creativity in adapting this recipe. The result is delicious, with a jolt of engaging flavor. Serve as a side dish or finger-food appetizer with your favorite sauce.

Ingredients

For stuffing:	For cover:
2 tsp/ 10 ml sesame seeds	2 tsp/ 10 ml oil
¼ cup/ 60 ml dry coconut, grated	½ tsp/ 2.5 ml cumin seeds
2 tsp/ 10 tsp poppy seeds	¼ tsp/ 1.25 ml turmeric
2 tsp/ 10 ml oil	¼ tsp/ 1.25 ml hing
¼ tsp/ 1.25 ml hing	1 tsp/ 5 ml red chili powder
½ tsp/ 2.5 ml turmeric powder	2 tsp/ 10 ml garlic paste
1 medium onion finely diced	1 tsp/ 5 ml salt divided into two parts
4 cloves garlic finely diced	1 cup/ 240 ml besan (chickpea flour)
½ tsp/ 2.5 ml salt	1 cup/ 240 ml boiling water
2 small green chili peppers or 1 medium chili, finely chopped	1 Tbsp/ 5 ml oil for frying
1 tsp/ 5 ml red chili powder	coconut or coriander leaves for garnish
½ tsp/ 2.5 ml garam masala	

6-8 servings · sesame · 40 min · 10 min · grinding equipment, steamer

Method

1. First prepare the spices for the stuffing. In a frying pan, dry roast sesame seeds, grated coconut, and poppy seeds. Stir and shake the pan for around 4-5 minutes until they are browned, dry and aromatic. Next, using a grinder or other grinding technique of choice, grind the mixture to a coarse powder.

2. Heat oil in a heavy frying pan or wok (kadai). Add hing, turmeric powder, onion, garlic and salt to taste and sauté on a medium-low flame so you don't burn the spices. Add chili peppers after around 2-3 minutes. When onions are golden brown, after around 5-7 minutes, mix in red chili powder, and garam masala. The mixture should be paste-like in texture.

3. Make the spice mixture for the dough by heating oil in a wok. Add cumin seeds, turmeric, hing, red chili powder, garlic paste, and ½ tsp salt. Cook for 2-3 minutes on a medium to low flame. Set aside.

4. Pour the besan (chickpea flour) into a mixing bowl. Add the garlic/onion and spice mixture. Very gradually add one cup of just barely boiling water, while mixing constantly and vigorously. You can also use an electric mixer with a dough hook. Add half a teaspoon of salt and continue to knead. After around 3-4 minutes, you should get a sticky dough that is soft to the touch. If the dough starts sticking to your hands, add a pinch of flour to your fingers and rub together into the bowl.

5. Take a plastic sheet or plastic wrap and grease lightly with oil. Roll out the dough evenly on it (approx ½ cm thick). Spread a layer of stuffing. Roll it gently and make a tight roll; this is the maswadi. Secure the ends by sticking well.

6. Steam the maswadi in one of two ways. The first way, which is the classic Maharashtrian method is as follows: Place the entire roll into a metal steaming pot (lightly oiled) or into a bamboo steamer, over an inch of boiling water. Steam for 10 minutes and then remove from steamer and place onto a board. Let it cool for 10-15 minutes or until it is easier to handle, and then slice the maswadi roll into pieces.

The second way, which is a variation on the classic method, is to slice the pieces before steaming them, as follows: Cut the roll into 1-inch slices, and then steam each piece in a bamboo steamer or a lightly greased metal mesh steamer, for 4-5 minutes each.

7. For a crispier result, you can then pan sear the steamed maswadi pieces in a skillet with a teaspoon of oil or ghee. The pan searing method should take 4-5 minutes on each side, or until it turns brown.

To garnish, top with coconut and coriander leaves. This dish is delicious just as it, or it may be served with chutney.

snacks and finger foods

puran poli

Sweet Stuffed Flatbread
by Indu Sona Mane

This Maharashtrian specialty of crisp dough stuffed with chickpeas and jaggery holds a special place in the hearts of the women of the collective. It is the food that brings back the most beloved memories of the village festivals of their youth. The sweet-savory snack reminds the women of communal get-togethers and the special foods that were served at these annual fairs. Serve it any time you want to fill up with sweet thoughts.

Ingredients

- **1 cup/ 240 ml** dry split chana dal (split chickpea lentils)
- **½ cup/ 100 gr** sugar
- **1 cup/ 240 ml** jaggery (sugarcane pulp)
- **1 Tbsp/ 15 ml** cardamom
- **½ tsp/ 2.5 ml** nutmeg
- **½ tsp/ 2.5 ml** fennel seeds
- **¼ tsp/ 1.25 ml** tsp saffron (optional)

For dough:

- **2 cup/ 256 gr** all-purpose white flour or whole wheat flour
- **2 Tbsp/ 10 ml** oil or ghee
- **¼ tsp/ 1.25 ml** salt
- **¼ tsp/ 1.25 ml** turmeric
- water
- oil or ghee for frying

Method

For puran (the filling):

1. Wash and soak chana dal in a generous amount of water for 4 hours.

2. Add chana dal to pressure cooker. Add 1 cup of water and pressure cook until 4 whistles or alternatively, cook chana dal on a low flame in a regular medium pot for an hour.

3. Mash the boiled chana dal and place in a heated pan over a low flame. Add sugar and jaggery and mix well. Keep stirring over the heat until the mixture becomes thick and starts to separate from the sides of the pan. It should take around 30-40 minutes.

4. Add cardamom powder, nutmeg, and fennel seeds and mix well. You may also add saffron here if you wish. Mix well for another 5 minutes.

For dough:

1. Place flour into a deep bowl. Add oil, salt and turmeric. Mix well.

2. Add water gradually as needed as you knead the dough. It should be loose and soft.

3. Cover and leave it to rest for 1 hour.

snacks and finger foods

6 servings | 5 hours | 30 min | 4 hours soaking dal

How to assemble the puran poli:

1. Mold the dough into balls, roughly 1-2 inches (4-5 cm) in diameter. Roll out a ball into a thick circle.

2. Take a small spoon full of the chickpea mixture and place it at the center of the puri. Roll up the dough around the stuffing and pinch it closed on top, and make sure it is completely sealed.

3. Heat up a frying pan on a medium heat. Add a dollop of oil or ghee. Place a puran poli into the pan and fry for 4-5 minutes on both sides until it gets nice golden spots. Flip with care so they do not fall apart.

Serve immediately, hot, with a dollop of ghee.

snacks and finger foods

mysore bhajji

Yogurt Fritters
by Jayshree Kondwal

Ah, the bhajjis. The women love their bhajjis, fried dumplings that can be filled with a wide variety of ingredients – vegetables, spices, greens, and cheeses. Not only are these snacks easy to make and inexpensive, they are also filling and delicious. This spicy yogurt variation makes a perfect snack or finger food, and is great for parties and lunchboxes alike. They are best dipped in coconut chutney, but can go with almost any chutney or sauce.

Ingredients

1 cup/ 128 gr all-purpose flour (maida)

½ tsp/ 2.5 ml baking soda

¼ cup/ 60 ml grated fresh coconut

1 Tbsp/ 15 ml sugar

½ tsp/ 2.5 ml salt

1 inch/ 2 cm ginger, grated

1 tsp/ 5 ml jeera (cumin seeds)

½ tsp/ 2.5 ml chopped coriander

2 small green chili peppers

1 cup/ 240 ml soft white cheese, either paneer, cottage cheese or ricotta

Method

1. In a large mixing bowl, combine flour, baking soda, coconut, sugar, salt, ginger, jeera, and coriander. Add chopped and deseeded chili peppers – and remember to use rubber gloves when handling them.

2. Add the cheese, and knead well. The dough should not need any liquid other than the liquid in the cheese. Set aside for 1-2 hours to rest.

3. When the dough is ready, make golf ball-sized balls out of the batter. Heat oil in a pan or pot, and deep fry the balls in oil until they are brown on all sides, around 4-5 minutes each. Turn in the middle. Remove the bhajjis from the oil with a slotted spoon and rest them on paper towels to continue to drain excess oil.

Serve with your favorite chutney.

 25-30 bhajjis

 coconut
 10 min
 20 min
 2 hour dough rest

snacks and finger foods

kamal shivaji kadam

Kamal, the 36-year-old mother of two from the Dheru village in the Satara district, was married at the age of 15. She stayed in school until the eighth grade but left because her father could not afford the education after that. Her family pulled her out of school, and she went to work in the fields with the rest of the clan.

Kamal really wanted to take her education further, and had every intention of getting back to studies. When she discovered that the family allowed her younger brother to stay in school, she was upset. "I nudged my mother a lot," she says. "I asked her why my brother got to stay in school and not me. But it didn't change anything." Instead of getting an education, she got married.

Today, Kamal has two children, a 20-year-old girl and an 18-year-old boy, who are both studying commerce.

Kamal misses her village. Even thinking about the village perks her up and brings out the fire in her eyes. "I miss working in the fields, even in the heat," she says, "because you are with everyone in the family. You have fun and enjoy each other's company. You go to the shade in the middle of the day and eat and make jokes."

She also misses the fairs, the friends, and the fresh air.

When Kamal first arrived in Kalwa nearly 20 years ago, there were no roads and it was impossible to get around. Now the road situation has gotten much better, but they still face problems with water and electricity. They only get water a few hours a day, and electricity only a few hours a day. The other main obstacle for her is hygiene and cleanliness. Although this, too, has gotten a bit better over the past twenty years, it is still a challenge.

Kamal learned how to cook right before she got married. Her mother taught her to make puran poli, a favorite dish that is also very tedious. "My mother told me that this is the most important food to learn because if you can master this, then you can master everything!"

Kamal contributed some delicious recipes to the cookbook, including methi samosas, coconut-cauliflower curry, capsicum-potato masala, and palak paratha, as well as the vibrant spice mix kanda lasun chutney and the drink aam panha.

Kamal dreams about returning to the farm in the village. Her husband not only pays the rent in their house in Kalwa but also pays to maintain the farm. Once her son and daughter are married, she hopes to return to the village – with her son's future family – where they can have a better life.

kanda bhajji

Onion Fritters
by Kamal Kadam

This fried-onion street food is a Mumbai favorite – easy, simple, inexpensive, and very satisfying.

Ingredients

2 cups/ 256 gr besan (gram flour)

1 tsp/ 5 ml salt or more to taste

1 Tbsp/ 15 ml oil for the batter

2 cups/ ½ liter thinly sliced onions (approximately 3 medium-large onions)

oil for deep frying

Method

1. In a large mixing bowl, combine besan, salt and oil.

2. Pour the onions into the flour and mix well, making sure that the onions are well-coated. The moisture from the onions should be enough to make a batter. There is no need to add water. Add more flour if the mixture is too moist. Set aside for 5 minutes to absorb.

3. Heat oil in a pot. Place a handful of coated onions into the oil and fry until they brown, around 4-5 minutes per batch. The oil should be very hot, but fry on a medium flame and not a high flame to make sure the onions cook inside. When they are done, remove onions with a slotted spoon and place on a paper towel to drain excess oil.

Sprinkle with salt, and serve hot with fried green chili peppers, spicy green chutney or ketchup.

snacks and finger foods

 2-3 servings   10 min 20 min

savory appam

Pancake Puffs
by Mangal Vittal Mane

Appam, fritters best described as pancake puffs or pastry balls, can be made sweet or savory. They are often prepared in special pans called appam patra, which are a cross between a frying pan and cupcake tins that are uniquely designed for this dish. If you do not have access to an appam patra (they are generally available in Indian shops and online), you can simply fry appes in ball-shapes in a regular frying pan. This version of the appe is savory and spicy. Serve hot for breakfast or as a snack and it goes nicely with coconut chutney.

Ingredients

- 1 cup/ 240 ml semolina
- ¾ to 1 cup/ 180-240 ml buttermilk
- pinch of baking soda
- 1 onion finely chopped
- ½ cup/ 120 ml chopped coriander leaves
- 2 Tbsp/ 10 ml minced green chili peppers
- 1 Tbsp/ 5 ml ginger paste
- 2 Tbsp/ 10 ml chopped curry leaves
- 1 tsp/ 5 ml cumin seeds
- ¼ tsp/ 1.25 ml salt (or more to taste)
- oil

Method

1. Mix together semolina, buttermilk and baking soda. Let sit for an hour.

2. After an hour add chopped onion, coriander leaves, chili peppers, ginger paste, curry leaves, cumin seeds and salt. Mix with spoon.

3. Grease appam patra or frying pan and heat.

4. If using an appam patra, put a ball of batter in each segment, like cupcakes. If using a frying pan, make individual balls and place into the pan.

5. Cover appam patra or frying pan with lid and cook one side of appe for 4-5 minutes over medium heat, until it browns. Turn over to the other side and cook on the other side.

Serve hot with coconut chutney.

15-20 appes | 1 ½ hours | 20 min | 1 hour pre-soaking | Appam patra (appe pan) if possible

upvas puri bhaji

Potato Topping for Crispbread (During "Upvas" or Fast)
by Usha Pimpre

This spicy potato stir fry is a "vrat" or "upvas" food that may be eaten during fasts. This dish accompanies the upva puris, special puris made out of the light amaranth flour instead of wheat, rice, or gram flour, which are all forbidden while fasting. Chili peppers give the dish a spicy kick to keep the digestive tract warm during fasting.

Ingredients

- **2 Tbsp/ 30 ml** ghee or oil
- **1 tsp/ 5 ml** jeera (cumin seeds)
- **1 tsp/ 5 ml** mustard seeds
- **4** green chili peppers, finely diced
- **1 tsp/ 5 ml** grated ginger
- **1 tsp/ 5 ml** salt
- **4 medium** boiled, diced potatoes
- **1 Tbsp/ 15 ml** sugar
- **1 Tbsp/ 15 ml** grated coconut
- **1 cup/ 240 ml** of finely diced coriander leaves
- **handful** of curry leaves

Method

1. Heat oil in a pan over high heat. Add jeera and mustard seeds, and heat until the mustard seeds "pop". Add chili peppers, ginger, and salt, and mix well for 2-3 minutes.

2. Add the diced potatoes and coat them with the spice mixture. Cook for five minutes, stirring constantly.

3. Add sugar and coconut and mix for another 3-4 minutes, or until all the flavors are blended.

4. Finally add coriander and curry, and mix for another 2-3 minutes.

Serve with upvas puris to accommodate fasters, or with regular puris on non-fasting days.

snacks and finger foods

2-4 servings   coconut   15 min   15 min   30 min boil potatoes

Methi Samosas

Fenugreek Pastries
by Kamal Shivaji Kadam

These stuffed, warm, savory pastries come in many varieties. This yogurt-fenugreek version has a classic Maharashtrian flavor. The samosas are best eaten fresh, but can be stored for 2-3 days in an airtight box and served at room temperature.

Ingredients

For the dough:

- **2 cups/ ½ liter** all-purpose wheat flour
- **1 tsp/ 5 ml** salt
- **1 tsp/ 5 ml** baking soda
- **2 Tbsp/ 30 ml** oil or ghee
- **1 cup/ 240 ml** water

For the filling:

- **1 Tbsp/ 15 ml** oil for frying
- **1 Tbsp/ 15 ml** mustard seeds
- **1 tsp/ 5 ml** cumin seeds
- **2 medium** potatoes, boiled
- **4 Tbsp/ 60 ml** paneer, or **1/3 cup/ 80 ml** yogurt
- **2 tsp/ 10 ml** salt
- **1 tsp/ 5 ml** turmeric
- **1 tsp/ 5 ml** garam masala
- **1 large** bunch of methi (fenugreek leaves), finely diced
- **2 cups or ½ liter** of oil for frying

Method

1. Make the dough. In a large mixing bowl, combine flour, salt, baking soda and oil. Drizzle in the water gradually as you knead, until you get a nice, soft dough. Set aside for half an hour while you prepare the filling.

2. Make the filling. In a frying pan, heat oil, and add mustard and cumin. Fry until the mustard seeds "pop" and remove from the heat. In a large bowl, mash the boiled potatoes along with the paneer, salt, turmeric and garam masala. Add methi and mix well. The filling should be creamy but firm.

3. Assemble the samosas. At this point, there are different methods for assembly. The traditional method calls for making round, flat shapes out of the dough, cutting each in half, and then folding the dough like a cone and then stuffing a teaspoon of filling into the cone, closing the top, and finally sealing the top with a dab of water.

There is a slightly easier method, illustrated in the accompanying photos, in which you roll out a vertical strip, place the stuffing on a corner, and then fold the strip one triangle at a time. Either method requires some practice, but they both create lovely triangle-shaped stuffed pieces.

Another tradition is for the samosas to be semi-circular and twirled on the edges. Roll out the dough into flat circles. Then place a bit of the mixture on one side and fold over into a half-moon shape. Then pinch the edges closed with a tiny twist of the thumb to create a rope-like effect along the edge. No matter how you shape the samosas, make sure that they are well-sealed.

 20 samosas   1 hour   30 min   30 min

Place the assembled samosas into a plate or bowl while they wait to be fried. You should end up with approximately 20 samosas, stuffed and sealed, and ready for frying.

4. Fry the samosas. In a deep pot or a wok, heat enough oil so that the oil is approximately 2-3 inches and enough to cover the samosas completely. Carefully place the samosas into the hot oil. A standard wok should hold 6-7 samosas comfortably at one time. Fry until the samosas turn brown, approximately 8-10 minutes. Turn them over halfway through to ensure an even browning.

5. Remove the samosas from the oil with a slotted spoon and rest them on paper towels to continue to drain excess oil.

Serve with tomato chutney, raita, or dips of your choice. They can be stored in an airtight box and keep for 2-3 days.

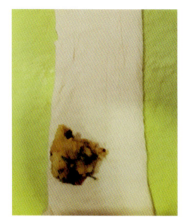
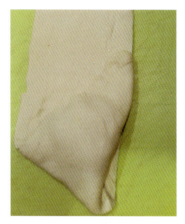

snacks and finger foods

alu wadi roll

Taro Leaf Cutlets
by Sangita Raut

This savory, rolled leaf snack unique to Maharashtra is made with taro (colocasia or alu) leaves and chickpea flour. If you cannot find taro leaves in your area, you can use large kale or spinach leaves as a substitute. Alu wadi rolls are considered a specialty and are traditionally served hot with tomato sauce. Or you can eat it as a snack along with your afternoon tea.

Ingredients

4-5 large taro leaves (colocasia, alu, kale or spinach)

2 cups/ 256 gr besan (chickpea flour)

1 cup/ 240 ml tamarind juice

1 cup/ 240 ml jaggery (sugarcane)

1 tsp/ 5 ml jeera (cumin seeds)

1 tsp/ 5 ml red chili powder

½ tsp/ 2.5 ml turmeric

salt to taste

oil for frying

Method

1. Wash the taro leaves (or substitute leaves) well. Dry the leaves with a towel or paper towel.

2. In a bowl, mix besan, tamarind juice, jaggery, jeera, chili powder, turmeric, and salt.

3. Rub the paste all over the leaves, and roll tightly.

4. Steam the roll for 15 minutes in a steamer over a pot with 1-2 inches of boiling water. You can use a bamboo steamer or a metal steamer. If using metal, make sure to oil the surface before placing the roll inside the steamer.

5. Cool in the refrigerator for 1-2 hours, or in the freezer for half an hour, to solidify.

6. When cool cut into ½ in or 1 cm slices.

7. Heat a frying pan with a bit of oil. When the oil is hot, pan fry each slice for 3-4 minutes on each side on a medium flame until the sides are brown.

Serve with tomato sauce.

 8-10 slices   2 hours 20 min bamboo or metal steamer

bharwa bhindi

Stuffed "Lady Fingers" or Okra
by Hirabai Vilas Umbarkar

These beautiful okras are stuffed with delicious spicy masalas. The stuffing ingredients vary, but this is a favorite Maharashtrian version. These can be served as an appetizer or a side dish, and go well with chapattis.

Ingredients

- **4 cups/ 1 liter** raw okra (the longer and thinner the better)
- **4 Tbsp/ 60 ml** neutral oil (e.g., sunflower oil or canola oil)
- **1 tsp/ 5 ml** cumin seeds
- **1 tsp/ 5 ml** fennel seeds
- **½ tsp/ 2.5 ml** hing
- **6** curry leaves
- **1** onion, chopped
- **3 tsp/ 15 ml** coriander powder
- **2 tsp/ 10 ml** red chili powder
- **1 tsp/ 5 ml** cumin powder
- **1 tsp/ 5 ml** amchur (dry mango powder)
- **½ tsp/ 2.5 ml** salt
- **¼ tsp/ 1.25 ml** turmeric powder

Method

1. Wash, clean and dry okra. Cut off the tips on both sides. Slit each okra without cutting through it completely, to make a pocket for the stuffing.

2. Heat a non-stick pan and add half the oil for frying. Add cumin seeds, fennel seeds, hing, and curry leaves. Sauté for fifteen seconds. Then add the chopped onion and cook until soft, about 5 minutes.

3. In a bowl, mix coriander, red chili, cumin, amchur, salt and turmeric. Mix all the spices well and add more oil as needed so the mixture just barely sticks together. Stuff each okra with a small spoonful of this spice mixture. You can dust the okras with the mixture if you have any leftover.

4. Add stuffed okra to cooked onion mixture and sauté gently keeping the masala spice mixture inside the okra. Cover with a lid and let the okra cook over a low heat for 10 minutes or until cooked through, stirring every few minutes to avoid burning at the bottom.

Serve with chapattis.

snacks and finger foods

4-6 servings

 20 min
 10 min

aloo samosas

Potato and Pea Stuffed Savory Pastries
by Gloria Spielman

Samosas are one of the most famous Indian snack foods that have successfully made themselves known around the world. And for good reason – these crispy, flavorful, stuffed pastries are not only delicious but can also be quite addictive. This recipe is from Gloria Spielman, a wonderful Indian cook who lives in Israel, who served as a consultant for this cookbook, and who is known around her community for her special recipe for samosas. Her expertise in samosas and other Maharashtrian fare was passed down to her from her Bombay-born mother who now lives in London. Gloria says that learning how to properly fold samosa dough is a lifelong journey.

Ingredients

For the dough:

2 cups/ 256 gr all-purpose flour

½ tsp/ 2.5 ml salt

6 Tbsp/ 90 ml neutral oil (e.g., sunflower or canola)

1 cup/ 240 ml water

For the filling:

3 Tbsp/ 45 ml ghee or oil

½ tsp/ 2.5 ml cumin seeds

1 tsp/ 5 ml black mustard seeds

½ tsp/1.25 ml fennel seeds

1 medium onion, diced

½ tsp/ 1.25 ml salt

1 inch/ 2 cm piece fresh ginger, peeled and diced

4 cloves garlic, diced

1 medium green chili pepper, diced

2 tsp/ 10 ml garam masala

2 tsp/ 10 ml ground turmeric

½ cup/ 120 ml peas, fresh or frozen

4 large potatoes, boiled and mashed

½ cup/ 120 ml diced coriander leaves

juice of one lemon

snacks and finger foods

20 samosas   1 hour   30 min   30 min

Method

1. To make the dough, mix together in a large bowl the flour, salt and oil. Gradually add the water as you continue to knead, until a dough is formed. Transfer the dough to a work surface and continue to knead. The dough should be soft and not sticky. Transfer the dough to an oiled bowl, cover with a damp towel, and let it rest for 30 minutes.

2. Meanwhile, prepare the filling. In a large frying pan, heat the oil on a medium to high flame. Add the cumin seeds, mustard seeds, and fennel seeds and heat until the mustard seeds pop, around 2-3 minutes. Add the onion and salt, and sauté for 2-3 minutes, until the onions begin to soften. Add the ginger, garlic, chili pepper, garam masala and turmeric, and mix well. Make sure the onions are well coated. Add the peas and sauté for 2-3 more minutes. Then add the potatoes and mash together well. Keep blending as the mixture comes together, for around 5 minutes. Add the coriander leaves and cook for 2-3 more minutes. Set aside. Add the lemon juice to the mixture and blend one final time.

3. To assemble the samosas, divide the dough into small balls, a little larger than a golf ball. At this point, there are different methods for assembly. The traditional method calls for making round, flat shapes out of the dough, cutting each in half, and then folding the dough like a cone and then stuffing a teaspoon of filling into the cone, closing the top, and finally sealing the top with a dab of water.

There is a slightly easier method, illustrated in the accompanying photos, in which you roll out a vertical strip, place the stuffing on a corner, and then fold the strip one triangle at a time. Either method requires some practice, but they both create lovely triangle-shaped stuffed pieces.

Another tradition is for the samosas to be semi-circular and twirled on the edges. Roll out the dough into flat circles. Then place a bit of the mixture on one side and fold over into a half-moon shape. Then pinch the edges closed with a tiny twist of the thumb to create a rope-like effect along the edge. No matter how you shape the samosas, make sure that they are well-sealed.

Place the assembled samosas on a plate or bowl while they wait to be fried.

4. Deep-fry the samosas. In a deep pot or a wok, heat enough oil so that the oil is approximately 2-3 inches high, enough to cover the samosas completely. Carefully place the samosas into the hot oil. A standard wok should hold 6-7 samosas comfortably at one time. Fry until the samosas turn brown, approximately 8-10 minutes. Turn them over halfway through to ensure an even browning.

5. Remove the pastries from the oil with a slotted spoon and rest them on paper towels to continue to drain excess oil.

Serve with tamarind sauce, your favorite chutney, or dip. They can be stored in an airtight box and keep for 2-3 days.

snacks and finger foods

"soup and study"

The women received stellar training in how to prepare large quantities of healthy, delicious soup. During the training, award-winning Chef Adam Shrinivas of the 5-star Meluha the Fern, an Ecotel Hotel in Mumbai, taught the women advanced tips and techniques to improve their skills and their soup repertoire. This was vital to enable the launch of the Soup and Study program at the Joshua Jacob Greenberger Learning Center in December 2017.

This new Center serves as a safe space for students to enjoy after school. Here, they are able to learn, play games, receive tutoring, and work on their homework. Between the hours of 2:30 and 5:30pm every day, children of primary school age use the Center to receive tutoring and extra support in school. From 6:00 to 9:00pm, students in grades 8-10 use the Center to study and relax in a warm, supportive environment.

The Center, located in the Bhaskar Nagar neighborhood in the heart of the Kalwa slum, a community of 200,000 residents, was named in in loving memory of GPM-Entwine fellow Joshua Jacob Greenberger who tragically passed away in May 2017. Josh devoted his time teaching the vulnerable children living in the slums with the 2013 volunteer cohort.

This program offers relief for Kalwa parents, who often have to choose between school and work for their young children. The program enables students to study and eat, and to stay in school rather than go out to dangerous, body-breaking and illegal labor. By staying in school, they can acquire a strong education, and ultimately get decent jobs to create a better future for themselves and their families.

"It is so meaningful for Josh's legacy to be a learning center that cares for children's education as well as their health and nutrition," said Josh's mother Mrs. Penny Greenberger, along with her husband, Mr. Bob Greenberger, of Cleveland, Ohio. "He loved children so much."

upvas rajgiria puri

Amaranth Crispbreads for Fasting
by Usha Pimpre

These puris are made from ingredients that are permitted while fasting. The flour base is amaranth, a light and very healthy leaf vegetable that acts like a grain. This amaranth puri dough has a firmer texture than flour and rice-based doughs and takes a bit longer to shape as well as to cook. It may not bubble in the oil quite the same way regular puris do, but they are still delicious, and can be a filling treat for fasters.

Ingredients

1 ½ cups amaranth flour

2 small boiled and mashed potatoes

½ tsp turmeric powder

¼ tsp ajwain (carom seeds)

½ tsp red chili powder

¼ tsp salt (rock salt for fasting)

water as needed for dough

oil for deep frying

Method

1. In a large bowl, mix the amaranth flour and mashed potatoes.

2. Add turmeric, ajwain, chili powder, and salt and mix well. Drizzle water as you mix, as is needed, until it becomes a soft dough. Knead well. Let the dough rest for 10 minutes.

3. Heat oil in a wok or deep pot over a high heat. Divide the dough into golf ball-size balls. Roll out and flatten into round disks.

4. When the oil is hot, carefully place the puris into the oil. Fry until they are brown, around 3-4 minutes, and then flip to the other side. When the puris are brown and crispy on both sides, remove from the pan and drain in a colander or on a towel.

snacks and finger foods

yields 8-10 puris

15 min

15 min

30 min (boil potatoes)

medu vada

Lentil Fritters
by Subhadra Khose

These donut-shaped fritters, crunchy on the outside and soft on the inside, are a favorite breakfast or snack food. Easy to make and a great way to use up leftover lentils, they go well with a wide variety of chutneys.

Ingredients

2 cups/ ½ liter urad dal (black gram lentils)

1 cup/ 240 ml rice flour

½ tsp/ 2.5 ml cardamom powder

pinch hing

handful coriander leaves, finely diced

¼ tsp/ 1.25 ml salt

3 Tbsp/ 45 ml sugar (optional)

water as needed

oil or ghee for deep frying

Method

1. Soak the dal for 3-4 hours. Drain, and then cook in water for about an hour until completely soft. Drain excess water, and mash the dal.

2. Place the blended dal in a mixing bowl. Add flour and all the spices, herbs, and salt and mix into a dough. Add sugar if you prefer a slightly sweeter taste. Add water if needed. The mixture should have a consistency between a batter and a dough, dry enough to form balls but still with the moisture of a fritter rather than a bread.

3. Heat oil in a wok or deep pan. Meanwhile, form donut-shapes out of the batter. When the oil is hot, place the vadis (fritters) into the oil. Cook on a high flame until the vadis are crispy on the outside, around 5 minutes.

Serve hot or room temperature as breakfast or a snack. These vadis go well with coconut chutney.

snacks and finger foods

8-10 pieces   1 hour   20 min   3-4 hours soaking dal

paneer pakoda

Cheese Fritters
by Usha Pimpre

These crunchy, deep-fried, paneer-stuffed savory snacks are a perfect pick-me-up, lunchbox filler or comfort food at the end of the day. They are perfect for dipping into tomato sauce or enjoying while sipping a hot cup of chai. And they are quick and easy to make too.

Ingredients

For the paneer:

1 cup/ 240 ml paneer, cubed (feta, Bulgarian and Halloumi cheeses are suitable alternatives)

1 tsp/ 5 ml ginger-garlic paste

½ tsp/ 2.5 ml red chili powder

1 tsp/ 5 ml salt (less if using a saltier cheese)

1 tsp/ 5 ml turmeric

For the batter:

1 cup/ 128 gr besan (gram or chickpea flour)

¼ cup/ 36 gr corn flour

½ tsp/ 2.5 ml salt

½ tsp/ 2.5 ml baking soda

½ tsp/ 2.5 ml turmeric powder

½ tsp/ 2.5 ml red chili powder

1 Tbsp/ 15 ml oil for batter

oil for deep frying

Method

1. Cut paneer into 1-inch or 2.5 cm cubes. Place in a mixing bowl and add ginger-garlic paste, red chili powder, salt, and turmeric. Toss the paneer in the mixture until the paneer is covered in spices.

2. In another bowl, pour in gram flour, corn flour, salt, baking soda, turmeric, and chili powder. Add a little water to form a smooth batter; make sure it is not too watery.

3. In a deep pot, heat oil for frying. Dunk the marinated paneer in batter, making sure each cube is coated. Then gently place in the oil and deep fry until golden brown, around five minutes. Remove and drain on paper towels or cloth.

Serve hot with tomato sauce or any sweet chutney.

snacks and finger foods

4-6 servings   10 min   20 min

kothimbir vadi

Coriander Fritters
by Rohini Mahamuni

This classic Maharashtrian finger-food made with generous amounts of coriander is delightful served hot with tomato sauce or chutney.

Ingredients

2 cups/ ½ liter diced coriander leaves

1 cup/ 128 gr besan flour (gram or chickpea flour)

1 tsp/ 5 ml diced ginger

1 tsp/ 5 ml minced garlic

2 medium green chili pepper, diced

1 tsp/ 5 ml grated jaggery (optional)

1 tsp/ 5 ml salt

3-4 Tbsp/ 50-60 ml neutral oil for frying

1 tsp/ 5 ml mustard seeds

1 tsp/ 5 ml sesame seeds

coconut or coriander leaves for garnish (optional)

Method

1. In a large mixing bowl, combine coriander leaves with besan, ginger, garlic, chili peppers, jaggery, and salt. Mix well. Drizzle in water as you mix, making sure there are no lumps. Continue mixing until it forms a moist and sticky dough, around ⅓ - ½ cup.

2. Heat 2 inches of water in a large steamer pot. Oil the bottom of the steamer if you are using a metal steamer.

3. Shape the dough into a long roll. Place it into a metal or bamboo steamer, and steam for 15 minutes. Set aside and let it cool for 15-20 minutes.

4. When the roll has cooled, slice it into 1-inch pieces.

5. Heat oil in large frying pan over high heat. Add the mustard and sesame seeds and heat until the seeds "pop". Then, place the wadis into the oil. Fry for 2-3 minutes on each side, or until lightly brown.

Garnish with grated coconut or coriander leaves, and serve with your favorite chutney or sauce.

10-15 vadis

sesame, coconut

20 min

40 min

steamer (metal or bamboo)

banana cutlets

by Usha Pimpre

Bananas are a favorite ingredient of vegans and vegetarians because it is a sweet binder, especially useful in dishes like cakes and cutlets. Here, bananas are mixed with sweet potatoes and nutmeg for a distinct and surprising flavor. The recipe calls for special "vrat" ingredients as well such as tapioca and millet, flours that are allowed during the fasting. These cutlets make a great lunchbox treat, and go well with ketchup or tomato sauce.

Ingredients

2 ripe bananas

2 potatoes, boiled and mashed

2 sweet potatoes, boiled or roasted, and mashed

2 Tbsp/ 30 ml nutmeg

2 Tbsp/ 30 ml tapioca flour

1 tsp/ 5 ml coriander powder

1 medium green chili pepper, diced

1 Tbsp / 15 ml minced ginger

¼ cup/ 120 ml millet

juice of half a small lime

½ - ¾ cup/ 120-180 ml water

oil for frying

Method

1. In a large mixing bowl, combine bananas, potatoes, and sweet potatoes. Add nutmeg, flour, coriander, green chili, ginger, millet, and lime juice. Drizzle in water to form a batter – not too watery.

2. In a large frying pan or kadai, heat a generous amount of oil over a high heat. Shape the batter into cutlets, and place them in the oil. Fry on each side until brown, around 4-5 minutes each.

Serve hot with tomato sauce, or your favorite chutney.

snacks and finger foods

10-12 cutlets   10 min   20 min   Boiling potatoes and sweet potatoes

Subhadra Khose

Subhadra, 41, has one 16-year-old son. This was not her original plan, and in fact having only one child is unusual for the women. For the first few years of her marriage, she did not conceive, and only after visiting a doctor did she become pregnant. This is not a topic that is easily discussed, and is often hidden away in women's secret whispers.

Subhadra considers herself lucky, though. She says that usually when women do not become pregnant, members of the family or the community can be mean. They may point fingers at the woman and blame her for not doing femininity correctly. That can be really hard on a woman who is struggling with her own feelings around body, motherhood, and marriage and has all of those social norms to contend with as well. But Subhadra's family was not like that at all. She says that nobody in her family – on either side – blamed her.

Subhadra describes her family as particularly kind. For example, girls are expected to learn how to cook from an early age from their mothers. But Subhadra's mother did not pressure her. "My mother told me that if I don't know how to cook, I shouldn't worry because my future mother-in-law will teach me." Still, she ended up learning how to cook from her mother from the age of ten. She has memories of her mother teaching her how to make vegetables and other dishes.

Subhadra also has village memories of sitting with 25-30 members of her family to eat. She misses that more than anything.

She also misses wedding season. Every year, during April and May – the Maharashtrian summer – is when the weddings take place. People return to their villages during that time and it is a huge celebration.

When Subhadra was a child, a wedding would last eight days. It includes a halad, in which the women bathe the bride in turmeric paste all over her body. This is followed by a series of puja ceremonies – one for the house, one for the wedding, and more. Then there is the wedding ceremony itself.

And of course, there is the food. Special wedding delicacies include sweets like gulab jamun and jalebi, as well as an array of main dishes – pulaws, biryanis, and curries – and naturally a range of chapatis and puris. "But the best part of this is the whole family coming together," she says wistfully.

These days, some of this tradition is eroding. The weddings are no longer eight days long but more like three days. Still, even if it's only three days of the family getting together, it is what she looks forward to all year long.

Subhadra contributed the delicious medu vada, shepu bhaji, and idlis to this cookbook.

Subhadra dreams about returning to her village. Her plan is that when her son gets married, they will all return to the village and enjoy their farm.

upvas masala idli

Fasting Sponge-Ball Snacks
by Subhadra Khose

These spicy, soft, doughy snacks are steamed and go well with a wide variety of hot chutneys and dips. This version, with a millet base, is a fasting food. Idlis can be eaten as a snack or a light, easy meal.

Ingredients

- **2 cups/ 256 gr** millet flour
- **½ tsp/ 2.5 ml** salt
- **½ tsp/ 2.5 ml** baking soda
- **½ cup/ 120 ml** yogurt
- **1 cup/ 240 ml** warm water
- **2-3** green chili peppers
- **1 tsp/ 5 ml** cumin powder
- **2 tsp/ 10 ml** chopped ginger
- **handful** fresh coriander

Method

1. In a large mixing bowl, combine the millet flour with salt and baking soda. Add yogurt and one cup of warm water and mix well until it forms a thick batter.

2. Add the chili peppers, cumin powder, and ginger and blend well. Let the batter sit for 15 minutes.

3. If you have an idli steamer pot, pour the batter into the grooves in the idli pans and cover over water for 10 minutes. If you do not have an idli steamer, you can use a cupcake pan. Preheat the oven to 180° C or 350° F. Place a bowl of water into the bottom rack of the oven to function as a steaming agent. Generously grease the cupcake pan and pour the batter into the cupcake holders. Steam in the oven for 15-20 minutes or until the batter has become firm and spongy.

Serve hot with chutney or yogurt.

snacks and finger foods

10-15 idlis   20 min   20 min   idli steamer or cupcake pan

chili mushroom pakora

Spicy Tempura-Fried Mushrooms
by Hayley Dsouza

These delicious fried dumplings are a perfect snack, side dish or appetizer. It is especially loved by kids, and can be dipped in tomato sauce or chutney.

Ingredients

½ cup/ 120 ml button mushrooms, finely chopped

1 medium onion, finely chopped

1-2 small red chili peppers, finely chopped

1 small green chili pepper, finely chopped

1 cup/ 240 ml bread crumbs

1 tsp/ 5 ml red chili powder

1 tsp/ 5 ml coriander leaves, chopped

2 Tbsp/ 30 ml corn flour

½ cup/ 120 ml grated cheese, such as mozzarella or cheddar

salt to taste

¼ cup/ 120 ml water

oil for deep-frying

Method

1. In a large mixing bowl, combine mushrooms, onions, red chili peppers, and green chili pepper. Add breadcrumbs, chili powder, coriander leaves, and corn flour and mix. Add cheese and salt and mix again.

2. Add ¼ cup water, or more if needed, to make a sticky dough. Make sure the dough is stiff and well-blended.

3. Heat oil in a deep pan or wok. Drop golf ball-sized portions of the batter into the oil and deep-fry till golden and crisp, around 4-5 minutes. Turn them over before you remove them to make sure they are evenly browned on all sides. Drain on a towel, paper towel, or in a colander.

Serve pakoras hot with tomato sauce or green chutney mayo (green chutney and a dash of mayo).

yields 25-30 pakoras

5 min

20 min

The main dishes are based on a variety of grains, pulses and vegetables – such as eggplant, okra, and spinach. They are full of rich color and spices and are best eaten fresh and hot.

mains

Carrot-Spinach Khichdi
Coconut-Cauliflower Curry
Anda Masala
Chana Masala
Potato Bhaji
Shepu Bhaji
Pav Bhaji
Egg Pulav
Moong Dahl
Capsicum Potato Masala
Kolhapur Vegetable Masala
Mattar Paneer
Palak Paneer
Fullower Batata Rassa
Bharli Wangi (Brinjal)
Vegetable Biryani
Tofu "Seafood" Curry
Vegan Seitan "Lamb" Curry
Chinese Pulav
Tofu "Fish" Masala

the statu in

The women of the collective are fairly representative of the status of women who come from remote rural villages in Maharashtra. They all left school in order to get married, they all stayed married, they all moved to Kalwa to follow their husbands' work prospects, and they are all completely financially dependent on their husbands – except for one woman whose husband died, so she is moving back to the village to be with her extended family. Their lives are stories that are exclusive to women. Their social, cultural and economic circumstances reflect the fact that they are women.

For some women, there are additional aspects of their lives that are impacted by their gender. Manisha described how she stopped going to school because she began menstruating. Her family did not have the knowledge or means to access sanitary products that would let her learn in school. According to a report by Nielsen Corporation, 25% of girls quit school when they begin menstruating because they have no sanitary facilities, and 88% menstruating women in India do not use any sanitary products during their period and use alternatives like pieces of rag, ash, sand and husk.[1] This is one of the biggest obstacles to equal education for girls in India, and the women of the collective have been directly impacted by this.

For other women, prioritizing boys' education over girls' education has been equally devastating. Indu is still angry that her parents took her out of school, as are other women, especially the women whose families allowed the boys to continue studying. According to the organization Educate Girls, some 2.5 million Indian girls have never been to school – in part because only 55% of schools have toilets for girls.[2] According to the 2011 census, women's literacy lags far behind that of men. For every 100 girls in rural India only a single one reaches twelfth grade.

These issues only begin to scratch the surface of the status of women in India. Sexual abuse is a rampant problem for women. While India boasts the lowest divorce rate in the world, some 45.5% of Indian women report experiencing some form of physical or sexual violence in their marriages. A survey by the World Vision Organization in India of 45,000 children ages 12-18 across 26 states in India found that one in every two children is a victim of child sexual abuse, and one in every five do not feel safe because of the fear of being sexually abused. Moreover, 98% of rapes of children are done by people who are familiar to the victims.[3]

1 Aditi Patwardhan, "Demystifying Menstruation: These Women Educate Rural Girls & Provide Eco-Friendly Sanitary Napkins", The Better India. https://www.thebetterindia.com/86434/project-baala-nitisha-sethia-soumya-dabriwal-menstrual-awareness-rural-india/
2 Jacqueline Bhabha and Anisha Gopi, Triggering Success: Innovative interventions for Promoting Educational Access in India, Harvard University Southeast Asia Institute, 2016 http://www.educategirls.ngo/pdf/Triggering%20Success%20Innovative%20Interventions%20to%20Promote%20Educational%20Access.pdf
3 One in every two children victim of sexual abuse, says survey. One in every five children do not feel safe because of the fear of being sexually abused. Hindustan Times, May 16, 2017 http://www.hindustantimes.com/india-news/one-in-every-two-children-victim-of-sexual-abuse-says-survey/story-spc4MsZTJsmjyrITZJep7L.html

Poverty exacerbates the issues of violence and sexual abuse. "When parents are too poor to afford suitable childcare and the child is assaulted whilst both parents are out working," writes Prita Jha[4] of Open Democracy. This vulnerability may be especially problematic in slums like Kalwa where neighbors are often loosely responsible for one another's children while parents work. Moreover, poverty can make reporting even more difficult. "Where family and community ties are very strong, sexual assault may or may not be reported to the police depending on a number of factors, the most important of these being the relative power of the perpetrator's family and community versus that of the survivor," Prita Jha adds.

One of the most shocking statistics about gender in India refers to femicide, the deliberate killing of female babies. A 2013 report[5] found that an Indian girl child aged 1-5 years is 75% more likely to die than an Indian boy, making India the worst country in the world for baby girls. Although these numbers may be coming down, recent reports from the United Nations Department of Economic and Social Affairs (UN-DESA) data for 150 countries shows that India and China are the only two countries in the world where female infant mortality is higher than male infant mortality. In India, there were 56 male child deaths for every 100 female, a number that has gotten progressively worse since the 1970s in India, even as Pakistan, Sri Lanka, Egypt and Iraq improved.

In all of these areas, there is growing awareness, research, some government intervention, NGO involvement, and grass-roots movement towards change. India, like the rest of the world, is growing more attuned to gender issues both on the ground and in formal structures. Many organizations, like Gabriel Project Mumbai, are working towards effecting real change for women and children across India.

The women in the collective, who are changing their own lives as well as their own awareness about social trends that surround them, are part of these cultural shifts. How these changes will impact their daughters and granddaughters – well, that is yet to be seen.

---

4   Jha Prita, What will it take to end child sexual abuse in India? Open Democracy 26 September 2017
https://www.opendemocracy.net/5050/prita-jha/ending-child-sexual-abuse-india
5   Female Literacy Rate -- Census of India http://censusindia.gov.in/2011-prov-results/data_files/india/Final_PPT_2011_chapter6.pdf

carrot-spinach khichdi

Carrot-Spinach Rice-Lentil Pilaf
by Indu Sona Mane

Khichdi, a lentil-rice mixture that can be made with virtually any vegetable combination, is considered a "perfect" protein for vegetarians, and is full of health benefits. This dish has a prominent place in Ayurvedic healing, and is often eaten as the main meal for days at a time. You can use vegetables in season, such as beans, peas, broccoli, zucchini, cauliflower, cabbage, or squash. You can also use extra water in the cooking and serve with some of the liquid in it as a kind of soup.

Ingredients

- **1 cup/ 240 ml** split mung dal lentils
- **1 cup/ 240 ml** basmati rice
- **1 Tbsp/ 15 ml** neutral oil
- **1 tsp/ 5 ml** jeera (cumin seeds)
- **1 tsp/ 5 ml** mustard seeds
- **1 tsp/ 5 ml** coriander seeds
- **1 medium** onion, diced
- **1 tsp/ 5 ml** salt
- **2 cloves** garlic, diced
- **1 tsp/ 5 ml** turmeric
- **1 cup/ 240 ml** diced carrot
- **1 cup/ 240 ml** chopped spinach

Method

1. Soak the lentils and rice in a large bowl of water for an hour. Rinse well.

2. In a large pot or kadai, heat oil over a medium flame. Add jeera, mustard seeds and coriander, and heat until the mustard seeds start to crackle, around 2-3 minutes.

3. Add onion, salt, garlic and turmeric, and sauté until the onions become translucent, around 4-5 minutes.

4. Add carrots and fry for 2 minutes.

5. Add the drained, rinsed rice and lentils, and stir until they are well-coated in the spice mixture. Next add 6 cups of water. Bring to a fast boil over high heat, then reduce the flame to low and cover the pot. Cook for 10 minutes or until there is only a bit of water left.

6. Add the spinach, and more salt according to your taste, and stir well. Cover the pot and cook for another few minutes, until the water is almost entirely soaked up. Turn off the heat and let it sit covered for 3-4 minutes before serving.

Serve hot. Can be topped with yogurt or raita.

6 servings   10 min   20 min   1 hour lentil soak

coconut-cauliflower curry

by Kamal Shivaji Kadam

One of the beautiful aspects of cooking with the women is the discovery of flavor combinations – often with easy, familiar ingredients – that fill your kitchen with incredible aromas. This curry is an example of that kind of experience. If you have never tried heating cinnamon sticks in ghee – or even regular butter – this is your chance to unearth that scent. Top it with cauliflower, peas, tomatoes and coconut milk, and you will create a mouth-watering main dish. It is easy, delicious, and healthy to boot!

Ingredients

- **1 Tbsp/ 5 ml** ghee
- **4** cinnamon sticks
- **1 medium** green chili pepper, chopped
- **3 medium** tomatoes, chopped
- **¾ cup/ 100 gr** green peas
- **1 large** cauliflower, broken into florets
- **2** chopped onions
- **1 tsp/ 5 ml** salt
- **1 tsp/ 5 ml** sugar
- **1 tsp/ 5 ml** garam masala powder
- **1 cup/ 240 ml** coconut milk

Method

1. Heat the ghee in a frying pan over medium to high heat. Add cinnamon sticks and green chili pepper, and let it cook for 3-4 minutes.

2. Add tomatoes, green peas, and cauliflower and cook for 2 minutes.

3. Add chopped onions and cook for 5 more minutes.

4. Add salt, sugar, garam masala and coconut milk. Cover and simmer for 10 minutes.

Serve hot with chapattis or puris.

 4 servings
 coconut
 5 min
 15 min

anda masala

Egg Curry
by Alka Harishchandra Gaikwad

Eggs are not actually considered a vegetarian food in India, but we kept it in this cookbook for the benefit of Western-style vegetarian eaters who consume eggs. This dish is delicious, and perfect for soaking up with some warm naan or any other bread.

Ingredients

5 eggs

4 Tbsp/ 60 ml neutral oil

1 medium onion, sliced

¼ tsp/ 1.25 ml tsp salt

½ cup/ 120 ml of dry flaked unsweetened coconut

1 tsp/ 5 ml kanda lasun masala

1 medium tomato, chopped

1 tsp/ 5 ml ginger, finely chopped

1 tsp/ 5 ml garlic, finely chopped

½ tsp/ 2.5 ml red chili powder

1 tsp/ 5 ml turmeric powder

2 tsp/ 10 ml paprika

½ cup to 1 cup/ 180-240 ml warm water

1 tsp/ 5 ml salt

coriander or parsley leaves for garnish

Method

1. Boil four eggs in a pot of water for 15 minutes.

2. While the eggs are boiling, heat 1 tablespoon of oil in a frying pan or wok, and add the chopped onion and salt. Fry over medium to high heat until golden brown, around 5 minutes. Add dry coconut and kanda lasun masala, and cook for another 3-4 minutes until coconut is toasted. It should have a pasty consistency. Set aside.

3. In a medium saucepan, heat remaining 3 tablespoon oil. Add tomato, ginger, garlic, red chili powder, turmeric, and paprika. Cook over medium to high heat for 3-4 minutes. Add coconut-onion paste to the saucepan and stir well so the flavors mix together. Add ½ cup to 1 cup of warm water. Bring to a boil and add 1 raw egg. Gently mix egg in the curry. Put a lid on the saucepan and let the egg cook for 2-3 minutes.

4. Peel the four boiled eggs, slice them in half, and add to the curry. Add salt. Cover saucepan and simmer on a low flame for 5 minutes.

Garnish with cilantro or parsley and serve with naan, chapatti or sliced bread.

4 servings — Coconut, eggs, sesame seeds — 20 min — 20 min

mains

healing malnutrition in babies

The women's food-preparation skills are put to important use in one of the most crucial struggles in the Kalwa slum: fighting malnutrition in babies and children.

The women, working with **The Dr. Gerald J. Friedman Infant Malnutrition Intervention Program** of Gabriel Project Mumbai, prepare a powerful nutritional mix – the universally acclaimed Integrated Child Development Program (ICDP) protocol for reversing severe and acute malnutrition in babies. The three-month comprehensive nutrition program helps kick-start the child's physical and cognitive development uses Hyderabad Mix and Ezee Paste, potent protein-based food treatments specifically designed to treat malnourished children. In this program, advocated by the United Nations, the World Health Organization, and other emergency relief organizations, children undergo weight and height checks, upper arm circumference measurements and other physical and cognitive development measures, in order to diagnose and treat malnutrition and bring them to full and robust health.

Hundreds of babies and children receive the nutritional supplements prepared by the women, who work in collaboration with the Shravan Health Center in the Bhaskar Nagar slum neighborhood in Kalwa. The clinic, which was opened by GPM in August 2015 in partnership with Doctors for You, provides a full range of medical services, primarily to children and mothers. These efforts enable this 200,000-member community to receive accessible, affordable, quality health care.

The malnutrition program was conceived by the doctors in the clinic, who were concerned about high incidences of malnutrition among their patients – a harrowing problem in the slums. According to the World Bank, the

prevalence of malnourished children in India is among the highest in the world and has dire consequences for the children. Malnourished children have more infectious diseases, such as pneumonia and tuberculosis, experience stunted physical and mental development and have higher mortality rates than children who receive proper nourishment.

In addition, parents in the Malnutrition ICDP program are offered intensive nutritional counselling in order to help families emerge from dangerous cycles of malnutrition.

The program is named in memory of Dr. Gerald J. Friedman, a New York-based physician who practiced medicine for over 55 years and specialized in diabetes, cardiology and internal medicine. During World War II, Dr. Friedman served as a young army doctor in the Solomon Islands in the Pacific and was struck by how severe malnourishment affects the growth and development of children. The Estelle Friedman Gervis Family Foundation, an organization named after Dr. Friedman's beloved sister, Estelle, made this program possible through their generous support. The Foundation provides support services for needy children, including children in orphanages, those with physical illnesses or disabilities, developmental delays, or in stressful life situations. "Both my uncle and my mother would have been very proud to support the Gabriel Project Mumbai program so that we may assist children in living full and productive lives with their families," says Foundation President, Barbara Gervis, Estelle's daughter.

The women received special training in how to prepare this mix. "We love being able to help heal the babies," said Indu, after the training. "This makes us very happy."

Chana Masala

Chickpea Stew
by Ranjana Ramchandra Gaiakwad

The chana bean, or chickpea, is a staple of the Maharashtrian diet, used in a variety of forms and variations. This Chana Masala is considered by many to be the most popular curry in India. In fact, this is one of the dishes that the women in the collective make for the children in the Love2Learn school in Kalwa every week. The recipe is fairly straightforward to make, though you have to remember to soak the beans overnight. This recipe is full of aromatic Maharashtrian flavors and has a nice spicy kick. Serve with chapattis or over rice, the way the children love to eat it.

Ingredients

1 ¼ cup/ 250 gr dry chickpeas, soaked overnight in a generous amount of water

½ tsp/ 2.5 ml baking soda

½ tsp 2.5 ml turmeric

2 Tbsp/ 30 ml neutral oil

2 tsp/ 10 ml whole cumin seeds

1 tsp/ 5 ml mustard seeds

4 fresh green chili peppers, chopped

2 tsp/ 10 ml fresh curry leaves

1 tsp/ 5 ml asafetida (hing)

1 tsp/ 5 ml finely chopped ginger

2 tsp/ 10 ml garam masala

2 tsp/ 10 ml ground coriander

1 tsp/ 5 ml turmeric

1 tsp/ 5 ml cumin

1 tsp/ 5 ml red chili powder

salt to taste

Method

1. Drain the soaked chickpeas and rinse well in a colander. Fill a medium or large saucepan with 6 cups of water, along with baking soda and turmeric. Bring to a boil, and add the soaked chickpeas. Cook for 1 ½ hours, or until chickpeas are thoroughly cooked.

2. When the chickpeas are done, heat oil in a frying pan over medium heat. Add cumin, mustard, chili peppers, curry leaves, hing, and ginger, and cook until fragrant, around 3-4 minutes.

3. Add the cooked chickpeas. Stir until the chickpeas are coated with spices. Add garam masala, coriander, turmeric, cumin and red chili powder and mix well. Sauté over medium heat for a minute and add salt to taste.

Serve over rice or with chapattis.

 4 servings   40 min   1 hour   overnight soack

mains

potato bhaji

Potato Stew
by Maya Kadu

This simple potato dish is a filling and flavorful light meal or side dish. It can be easily doubled to accommodate a larger group.

Ingredients

- 4 **medium-sized** potatoes
- 2 **Tbsp/ 60 ml** neutral oil
- 1 **tsp/ 5 ml** cumin seeds
- 1 **tsp/ 5 ml** mustard seeds
- 1 **inch/ 2.5 cm** ginger, peeled and finely chopped
- 2 **cloves** garlic, peeled and chopped
- 1 green chili pepper, chopped
- 6 curry leaves
- 1 **large** onion, chopped
- 1 **tsp/ 5 ml** ground turmeric
- 1 **tsp/ 5 ml** salt
- ½ **cup/ 120 ml** fresh coriander, chopped

Method

1. Boil the potatoes in a pot of water until they are cooked completely, about 20 minutes. Peel and chop the potatoes into cubes and set aside.

2. In a frying pan, heat oil over medium to high heat. Add cumin and mustard seeds. Fry until the seeds crackle.

3. Add the ginger, garlic, green chili pepper, and curry leaves and fry for a minute. Add the chopped onion. Fry until it becomes soft and transparent. Add the turmeric and stir not allowing the turmeric to burn.

4. Add the chopped potatoes, salt and half of the cilantro leaves. Let the bhaji simmer for 5-6 minutes on a low flame, stirring occasionally.

Garnish with the remaining cilantro. Serve hot with poories, chapatis or dosas.

 2-4 servings   10 min   40 min   30 min boiling potatoes

shepu bhaji

Dill Stew
by Jayshree Chavdry

This stew, with its inimitable dill flavoring, makes a lovely light meal on a summer day.

Ingredients

- 1 cup/ 240 ml yellow moong dahl (lentils)
- 1 Tbsp/ 15 ml oil
- 1 tsp/ 5 ml mustard seeds
- ½ tsp/ 2.5 ml cumin seeds
- 1 medium onion, finely chopped
- 3 small green chili peppers, finely chopped
- 1 tsp/ 5 ml turmeric powder
- 2 cups/ ½ liter water
- 1 cup/ 240 ml finely chopped dill
- 3 cloves garlic, crushed
- salt to taste

Method

1. Soak the dahl in water for 20-30 minutes. Then rinse well.

2. Heat oil in a wok or medium saucepan over medium to high heat. Add mustard seeds, and fry until they begin to crackle. Add cumin seeds and chopped onions. Mix well and let cook for 2 minutes. Add chili peppers and cook for 2 more minutes.

3. Drain and rinse the presoaked moong dahl. Add turmeric and moong dahl to the pan, along with 2 cups of water and mix well. Cover the pan and allow the moong dahl to cook for 10-15 minutes or until fully cooked. Be careful not to burn the dahl and add more water if necessary.

4. Add the dill, garlic, and salt to taste. Cook covered for another 5-10 minutes.

Serve hot with dahl/rice or puris.

4 servings — 10 min — 30 min — 30 minutes to soak lentils

pav bhaji

Stew Served on Buns (Pav)
by Indu Sona Mane

This popular street food is enjoyed throughout Maharashtra, especially in Mumbai. The thick vegetable stew is packed with color and nutrients, and is usually served with "pav" or toasted buns.

Ingredients

2 cups/ ½ liter cubed potatoes, carrots and cauliflower, in any combination

1 Tbsp/ 15 ml neutral oil

1 large onion, chopped

1 tsp/ 5 ml salt

1 tsp/ 5 ml ginger, minced

1 tsp/ 5 ml garlic, minced

2 green chili peppers, diced

1 tsp/ 5 ml red chili powder

½ cup/ 120 ml peas

½ cup/ 120 ml green beans

1 bell pepper (capsicum), chopped

3 tomatoes, chopped

3 tsp/ 15 ml pav bhaji masala powder or garam masala

½ tsp/ 2.5 ml turmeric powder

1-1½/ 240-360 ml cups of water

½ tsp/ 2.5 ml lemon juice

salt to taste

2 buns

Method

1. In a large pot of salted water, boil the potatoes, carrots and cauliflower until cooked but not mushy, around 10-15 minutes.

2. While the vegetables are boiling, heat oil in a large pan. Add onions, salt, ginger, garlic and green chili peppers, red chili powder, and sauté until golden brown.

3. Add peas, green beans, bell pepper, and tomatoes, and sauté for 2-3 minutes.

4. Add boiled vegetables and sauté for 2-3 minutes until vegetables are well-coated.

5. Add pav baji masala and turmeric. Add 1-1 ½ cups of water to coat the vegetables; be careful not to turn it into a soup. Bring to a boil, cover, and simmer for 10 minutes, later adding a bit more water if needed.

6. Mash all the vegetables with the back of wooden spoon in the pan, until the mixture is pulpy. Add lemon juice and salt to taste.

Serve hot on toasted pav buns and spread with butter.

4-6 servings   20 min   20 min

mains

Egg Pilaf
by Victoria Mendes

This quick, easy, one-pot meal (pronounced "pull-OW", sometimes spelled "pulao") is an egg-based dish, which is not considered a vegetarian dish in India. It was contributed by Victoria Mendes, a GPM staffer, who helps manage the Delicio kitchen. Feel free to vary the vegetables depending on what is in season.

Ingredients

- **6** eggs
- **2 cups/ 400 gr** basmati rice
- **1 Tbsp/ 15 ml** neutral oil
- **3 medium** onions, finely chopped
- **1 tsp/ 5 ml** salt
- **1 clove** garlic, minced
- **½ inch/ 1 cm** ginger, minced
- **1 small** green chili pepper, finely chopped
- **2 medium** tomatoes, diced
- **1 Tbsp/ 15 ml** cumin powder
- **1 Tbsp/ 15 ml** turmeric powder
- **1 tsp/ 5 ml** garam masala powder
- **1 tsp/ 5 ml** coriander powder
- **½ tsp/ 2.5 ml** chili powder
- **8** curry leaves
- **½ cup/ 120 ml** mint leaves
- **1 cup/ 240 ml** whole milk yogurt
- **4 cups/ 1 liter** of water
- **½ cup/ 120 ml** cilantro leaves

Method

1. Hard boil the eggs in a pot of boiling water for 15 minutes. While the eggs are boiling, soak the rice in water and chop the vegetables for the next step. When the eggs are boiled, rinse them in cold water so that you can handle then and then peel the eggs.

2. Heat oil in a large pot over high heat. Add onions and salt, and cook until they turn golden brown, around 4-5 minutes. Add garlic, ginger, chili pepper, and tomatoes. Stir for a moment, then add the cumin, turmeric, garam masala, coriander, and chili powder. Stir well so that the vegetables are well coated in spices. Add the curry leaves and mint leaves and cook for 2-3 minutes until it is well blended.

3. Whisk in the yogurt and bring to a boil. Stir continuously.

4. Rinse the rice and add to the pot. Mix well so that the rice is coated with flavors. Then, gently place the eggs on top of the rice, and then pour water over the mixture. It should cover the rice by approximately ½ inch; adjust the amount if necessary. Bring to a boil and then simmer over a low heat for 10 minutes. Check to see if the rice is cooked and the liquid is soaked up. Add more water if needed. Gently fluff the rice with a fork while taking care not to break the eggs and cover. Let the pulav rest for a few minutes before serving.

Garnish with cilantro leaves or sprinkle with paprika.

6 servings

eggs

15 min

25 min

moong dahl

Lentil Stew
by Ranjana Ramchandra Gaikwad

This warm, filling dish, which can be made using different varieties of lentils, is a staple in Kalwa as well as much of India. The women of the collective make variations of dahl once a week for the children studying in the Love2Learn school. It can be served over rice or with chapattis or rotis.

Ingredients

- **1 cup/ 240 ml** moong dahl (split mung beans or yellow split peas)
- **6 cups/ 1.5 liters** of water
- **2 Tbsp/ 30 ml** oil
- **1 tsp/ 5 ml** mustard seeds
- **1 tsp/ 5 ml** cumin seeds
- **2-3** curry leaves
- **1** green chili pepper, chopped
- **1** onion, chopped
- **1** tomato, chopped
- **3 cloves** garlic, chopped
- **½ tsp/ 2.5 ml** turmeric
- **½ tsp/ 2.5 ml** ground cumin
- **1 tsp/ 5 ml** salt

Method

1. Soak the moong dahl for at least two hours. Drain and rinse.

2. In a medium saucepan, boil 6 cups of water. Add the dahl, lower the heat, cover, and simmer until the lentils are soft, around 45 minutes. Stir frequently.

3. While the dahl is cooking, heat oil in a frying pan over medium heat. Add mustard seeds, cumin seeds, curry leaves, and chili pepper. Let the spices "pop" for 1-2 minutes. Next add onions, tomatoes and garlic. Mix well, making sure the vegetables are coated in spices. Cook until onions are lightly browned, around 6-7 minutes.

4. When the dahl is ready, add the stir-fry to the pot. Add the turmeric, cumin, and salt. Cook on a low flame for 5 more minutes until the flavors are well-blended.

Serve with rice or rotis.

4 servings   10 min   45 min   2 hours to soak lentils

capsicum potato masala

by Kamal Shivaji Kadam

The secret to this warm, potato stew is the addition of cloves and cinnamon. These spices give the dish a feisty and stirring aroma. This dish is perfect for a light winter supper.

Ingredients

- 3 Tbsp/ 45 ml neutral oil
- 1 tsp/ 5 ml cumin seeds
- 1 tsp/ 5 ml mustard seeds
- 2 cups/ ½ liter of diced potatoes
- 3 medium green or red bell peppers (capsicums), diced
- 2 tsp/ 10 ml red chili powder
- 1 tsp/ 5 ml amchoor powder
- 1 tsp/ 5 ml ground cloves
- 1 tsp/ 5 ml ground cinnamon
- salt to taste

Method

1. Heat oil in a frying pan. Add cumin and mustard seeds and sauté until the seeds "pop", around 2 minutes.

2. Add potatoes, and coat in oil and seeds. Cook for 15 minutes, stirring regularly so that the potatoes do not stick to the pan. Add more oil if necessary.

3. Add bell peppers and the remaining spices including red chili powder, amchoor, cloves, and cinnamon. Cook until the potatoes are fully cooked, around 15-20 minutes, stirring constantly. Add salt to taste.

 2-4 servings   10 min 30 min

Kolhapur Vegetable Masala

by Indu Sona Mane

The historic city of Kolhapur in Maharashtra is known for its aromatic cuisine and is named in this masala. This flavorful vegetable stew can be served with rotis or over rice.

Ingredients

- **2 Tbsp/ 30 ml** oil
- **1 large** onion, diced
- **¼ cup/ 60 ml** chopped curry leaves
- **½ tsp/ 2.5 ml** turmeric
- **2 Tbsp/ 30 ml** garam masala
- **1 tsp/ 5 ml** red chili powder
- **1 tsp/ 5 ml** ginger-garlic paste
- **2 tomatoes or ½ cup/ 120 ml** of tomato paste
- **3 cups/ 720 ml** of vegetables of your choice (carrot, zucchini, sweet potato, squash, celery, turnip, pumpkin, cabbage, broccoli, cauliflower, etc) cubed into ½ inch pieces
- **½ cup/ 120 ml** fresh ground coconut (optional)
- **1 cup/ 240 ml** of water
- **½ tsp/ 2.5 ml** salt (or more to taste)
- **handful** of coriander leaves, finely diced

Method

1. In a medium-size pot, heat oil over high heat. Add onion and sauté for 2-3 minutes. Add the curry leaves, turmeric, garam masala and chili powder. Sauté for 4-5 minutes or until the onions are soft.

2. Add ground ginger/garlic paste, tomatoes or tomato paste, and the chopped vegetables. Mix well so that the vegetables are well-coated in spices and oil.

3. Add approximately 1 cup of water to cover the vegetables, coconut (optional) and salt.

4. Cook till veggies are soft. Add salt to taste.

Garnish with coriander leaves. Serve hot with rotis, chapattis, or rice.

 4-6 servings   15 min 30-40 min

mains

mattar paneer

Peas and White Cheese
by Sangita Raut

The nutty pea-cheese combination in this dish is a Maharashtrian favorite. The fried paneer cubes that are crisp on the outside and melting on the inside make for a delicious and filling meal.

Ingredients

3 Tbsp/ 45 ml of oil or ghee, divided throughout the recipe

1 cup/ 250 gr paneer, cubed

10 cashew nuts

1 large onion, chopped

¼ tsp/ 1.25 ml salt

2 Tbsp/ 30 ml ginger-garlic paste

1 tsp/ 5 ml turmeric

4 plum tomatoes, peeled and diced

½ cup/ 120 ml water

1 tsp/ 5 ml cumin seeds

1 tsp/ 5 ml mustard seeds

1 small green chili pepper

1 cup/ 240 ml mattar (peas), fresh or frozen

1 tsp/ 5 ml coriander powder

1 tsp/ 5 ml red chili powder

2 tsp/ 10 ml garam masala

1 tsp/ 5 ml amchur powder

¼ cup/ 60 ml yogurt or ricotta cheese

2 Tbsp/ 40 ml coriander leaves, finely diced

Method

1. In a large frying pan, heat 1-2 teaspoons of oil. Add the paneer cubes and shallow fry them on a medium flame until they turn brown on all sides, around 4-5 minutes. Continuously flip the paneer so they do not burn on any one side. Set the paneer aside, but keep the oil in the pan.

2. Add a bit more oil or ghee to the pan if necessary, and fry the cashews nuts on a medium to high flame until they are brown, around 4-5 minutes. Set aside but keep any remaining oil for the next step.

3. After adding more oil or ghee, if needed, to coat the bottom of the pan, add the onion and salt and sauté for 2-3 minutes. Add ginger-garlic paste, turmeric and coat the onions well. Add the tomatoes and cook for another 5 minutes or until the tomatoes have softened. Blend the onion-tomato mixture along with the cashews in a food processor or blender until it becomes a liquidy paste. Add up to ½ cup of water if necessary.

4. In a medium saucepan, heat enough oil or ghee to cover the bottom of the pan. Add the cumin and mustard seeds and heat until they "pop", around 2 minutes. Then add the green chili pepper and peas and sauté for another few minutes on medium heat until the peas and chili peppers soften. Next add the onion-tomato-cashew paste, along with the rest of the powder spices – coriander, red chili powder, garam masala, and amchur. Cook on a low flame for 5 minutes until the spices are well blended.

5. Add paneer cubes and mix well. Finally, add the yogurt and cook for 10 minutes on a low flame while stirring occasionally so it does not burn. Right before serving, add the coriander leaves.

Serve immediately, and is delicious as is or served with chapattis.

2-3 servings — cashews — 15 min — 25 min — blender or food processor

mains

kalpana gawde

Kalpana is from the village of Akeyand in the Satara district of Maharashtra. She says she is roughly 37 years old, though her exact age is unclear. Her oldest child is 21 and she was married, she thinks, at the age of 19.

Though the math clearly does not add up for the dates of the most significant events in Kalpana's life, I begin to understand that the women's ages are not always recoded or remembered as part of their life stories. But Kalpana also, shares that she cannot add numbers so that something so basic as narrating her own life story becomes a challenge. Like many village girls in India, Kalpana only stayed in school through first grade and therefore does not know how to read, write, or do basic math. Thankfully today, this has changed in many parts of India.

In the end, Kalpana's children – all of whom are now receiving excellent educations – help us resolve the dates in her life narrative. With their help, we are now fairly certain that she got married at the age of 15 and is now, indeed, 37 years old.

Kalpana and her husband moved their family to Mumbai ten years ago "for the children's education…there were no schools in the village." The contrast between her own story and that of her children is striking, and paints a phenomenal story of mobility, migration, and the power of women to change their children's lives. She has four children ages 12, 17, 19 and 21. Her son is studying to be an engineer, and all of her children are in school. She wants all of them, both her sons and daughters, to study well and get good jobs. "Of course, also get married," she adds quickly. But her biggest dream for them is to have the kind of economic stability that comes from getting a good education leading to professions where they will earn a high salary. Thus far, they are all on that track, thanks to the determination and willpower of their mother.

But there are things Kalpana misses about village life – like "being in the sun." She remembers how her family would be out in the fields all day growing potatoes, rice, strawberries, onions, and more. She misses the fields, the fresh food, and the clean air.

She also misses her extended family although is fortunate to have a sister living in Mumbai. "When I first came, I missed my family terribly," she recalls. She was homesick, lonely, and on her own. But since joining the women's collective, she has made friends and found her place. "We get together, we talk and we cook." Clearly, the role of the collective has been transformative to her.

She would like to move to a better place herself, but her dreams have transferred to her children. If her children are able to build better lives for themselves, she will be happy.

Kalpana contributed some delicious recipes to the cookbook: aloo paratha, raw tomato chutney, karwande lonche kala chana amti and palak paneer. Everything she knows about cooking, she says, she learned from her mother.

palak paneer

Spinach and White Cheese Stew
by Kalpana Gawde

This spinach-yogurt dish, which can be made with pureed or chopped spinach and garnished with your favorite cheese, is delicious on its own or with naan, parathas, or chapattis.

Ingredients

- 1 cup/ 240 ml spinach, chopped
- 1 green chili pepper, chopped
- 1 inch/ 2.5 cm ginger
- 2 cloves garlic
- 1 tsp/ 5 ml oil
- ½ tsp/ 2.5 ml cumin seeds
- 1 tsp/ 5 ml turmeric
- ½ cup/ 120 ml onion, finely diced
- 1 tsp/ 5 ml coriander powder
- 1 tsp/ 5 ml garam masala
- 1 tsp/ 5 ml salt
- 8 oz/ 250 gr paneer, cubed

Method

1. Boil a pot of water and cook the spinach for 2-3 minutes. Drain the spinach and blend green chili pepper, ginger and garlic in a blender or food processor. Drizzle water to aid in the blending process, but not too much that will make it too liquidy. It should form a paste.

2. In a frying pan, heat the oil over a high heat. Add cumin seeds, turmeric, and onions. Cook over a medium heat until the onions are brown, approximately 6-7 minutes.

3. Add spinach paste, coriander powder, garam masala and salt, and cook for 5 minutes.

4. Add paneer. Cook for five minutes.

Garnish with cheese.

TIP: For a delicious, slightly smoky flavor, shallow fry the paneer in oil until it gets brown on all sides, and then add it to the masala.

3-4 servings | 40 min | 10 min | blender or food processor

fullower batata rassa

Cauliflower-Potato Stew
by Rohini Mahamuni

This simple and easy vegetable stew is perfect for a light dinner, served over your favorite grain or with your favorite bread.

Ingredients

- **1 Tbsp/ 15 ml** neutral oil
- **½ tsp/ 2.5 ml** mustard seeds
- **½ tsp/ 2.5 ml** cumin seeds
- **pinch** of hing
- **6** curry leaves
- **1 inch/ 2.5 cm** ginger
- **3 cloves** garlic, chopped
- **2 medium** onions, chopped
- **1** tomato, chopped
- **½ tsp/ 2.5 ml** coriander
- **½ tsp/ 2.5 ml** cumin powder
- **½ tsp/ 2.5 ml** turmeric
- **½ tsp/ 2.5 ml** garam masala
- **1 tsp/ 5 ml** salt
- **2 medium** potatoes, cubed
- **2 cups/ ½ liter** of cauliflower florets
- **2 cups/ ½ liter** water
- **½ tsp/ 2.5 ml** jaggery
- **1 Tbsp/ 15 ml** dry grated coconut

Method

1. Heat oil in a large pan. Add mustard seeds, cumin seeds, hing, and curry leaves. Cook until the seeds "pop", around 2-3 minutes.

2. Add ginger, garlic, onions, and tomatoes. Stir well so that the onions and tomatoes are covered in spices. Let it cook for 2-3 minutes. Then add the coriander, cumin powder, turmeric powder, garam masala, and salt. Cook until the onions are translucent.

3. Add potato cubes and cauliflower florets, along with two cups of water. Bring to a boil, then lower the heat, cover, and simmer on low until the vegetables are cooked around 10 minutes.

4. Finally add the jaggery and coconut. Reduce heat and cook for an additional 3-4 minutes while stirring.

Serve hot with dahl, rice, grains, breads or puris.

 4 servings   coconut 10 min 15 min

mains

bharli wangi

Stuffed Baby Eggplants
by Rohini Mahamuni

This pretty dish of baby eggplants (brinjal) stuffed with a coconut, peanut and red chili paste is a favorite of many of the women of the collective. Subhadra Khose says this is her family's favorite dish, and she explains that the key to the brinjal is in the masala. If the masala is right, the dish will come out mouth-watering! This dish makes a particularly decorative starter, side, or light dinner. It looks much more complicated to prepare than it actually is! The women of the collective say it is best served with bhakris and chapattis.

Ingredients

2 Tbsp/ 30 ml grated coconut

4 tsp/ 20 ml roasted peanuts (crushed)

1 tsp/ 5 ml red chili powder

1 tsp/ 5 ml salt

8-10 small brinjal (eggplants)

4 tsp/ 20 ml oil

½ tsp/ 2.5 ml cumin seeds

½ tsp/ 2.5 ml mustard seeds

2 cups/ ½ liter water

2 tsp/ 10 ml tamarind juice

2 tsp/ 10 ml jaggery (sugarcane pulp)

1 tsp/ 5 ml salt

coriander or curry leaves and grated coconut for garnish

Method

1. Prepare stuffing mixture in a bowl by mixing together coconut, crushed peanuts, red chili powder and salt with a few teaspoons of water – just enough to make the mixture stick together.

2. Wash the brinjal. Then, without removing the green top, slice each in half lengthwise, and then again slice it in half lengthwise, so that there are four sections coming out of the top, like pedals coming out of a flower stem. The result is that the eggplant is sliced in four directions but held together in one piece by the stem.

3. Using your fingers or a small spoon, insert a spoonful of stuffing into each eggplant.

4. Heat oil in large frying pan. Add cumin and mustard seeds and let them heat until the seeds "pop", around 3 minutes. Then, place the stuffed brinjals into the pan. Pour two cups of water over them, as well as any leftover stuffing, and bring to a boil. Lower the heat, cover, and cook for 10-12 minutes, until the insides of the eggplant are cooked. You can tell when they are cooked because they turn darker and lose their white sponginess. Add tamarind, jaggery, and salt to the sauce, and cook for 3-4 more minutes.

Serve hot, garnished with coriander or grated coconut with rotis.

4-6 servings | coconut, peanuts | 10 min | 20 min

mains

Vegetable Biryani

Rice-Vegetable Pilaf
by Maya Kardu

This classic rice-and-veggie main dish is a favorite among many women of the collective. For Indu, for example, biryani is the go-to dinner in her house. This dish can be made with a variety of different vegetables, depending on seasons and availability. It can also be made in a pressure cooker for faster cooking. Top with chutney, raita, or dried fruit.

Ingredients

3 cups/ 720 ml vegetables in any combination: potatoes, sweet potatoes, peas, carrots, cauliflower, broccoli, beetroot, cubed

3 Tbsp/ 45 ml oil

1 tsp/ 5 ml mustard seeds

1 Tbsp/ 15 ml jeera (cumin seeds)

1 tsp/ 5 ml chili powder

1 tsp/ 5 ml turmeric

1 Tbsp/ 15 ml ginger-garlic paste

1 medium green chili pepper, finely chopped

1 onion, diced

1 tsp/ 5 ml salt

2 medium tomatoes, diced

2 cups/ ½ liter of cooked basmati rice

dried fruit, almonds, or cashews for garnish

Method

1. Parboil the vegetables in a pot of boiling water for 5-10 minutes to soften them. Set aside.

2. Meanwhile, in a large pot or pressure cooker, heat the oil. Add mustard and cumin seeds and wait for the seeds to "pop". Then, add the chili powder, turmeric, ginger-garlic paste, and chili pepper and mix well. Add the onions and salt, and sauté for a few minutes until the onion softens.

3. Add the tomatoes and allow to cook for 1-2 minutes.

4. Add all the vegetables, and just enough water to allow it to cook, but not too much that the dish becomes too liquidy – approximately 1-2 cups. Allow the vegetables to cook more until soft but not mushy, around 10 minutes.

5. When the vegetables are done, add the cooked rice and stir for another 2-3 minutes mixing all the flavors.

Garnish with dried fruits or nuts, top with yogurt, or it's delicious just out of the pot.

  6 servings   almonds, cashews 20 min 20 min 20 min cooking rice pressure cooker (optional)

mains

ragini godbole

Ragini is unique among the women of the Kalwa collective because she is the only one who was born in Mumbai. Unlike the other women, her parents were the ones who migrated from the village of Ratnagiri, a port city on the Konkan coast, known for its fabulous mangoes.

Ragini, 35, got married at the age of 17 to a carpenter and they have three children ages 17, 19, and 22. The oldest is studying computers, the middle child is a professional photographer, and the youngest is still in school.

Once a year, Ragini travels to Ratnagiri, which she really enjoys because she misses her family dearly and loves eating the local fruits. As she and I sit on the floor with the other women of the collective, Ragini explains that she learned how to cook from her mother-in-law. All of the women laugh in surprise because her own parents never allowed her to work and treated her like a princess; she never even knew how to make tea.

Since then, Ragini has become an expert cook. Before joining the Masala Mamas, she worked as a cook in other settings. But Ragini especially loves working with the women of the collective. "Most of the women are from different villages and I enjoy hearing their stories and learning about where they came from."

Ragini also talks about how the women support one another. "We resolve one another's troubles", she says. "We talk to each other and help each other."

Ragini contributed many recipes to this cookbook – especially the mango-based drinks such as mango lassi and jal jeera. She was also one of the few women to contribute fish or lamb recipes. We converted Ragini's non-veg recipes to veg, using ingredients such as soy, seitan, and tofu.

Ragini is a much beloved member of the Masala Mamas group. Her easy smile, quick humor, and bright eyes always liven up the group and bring people together in laughter.

tofu "seafood" curry

by Ragini Godbole

This recipe originally called for prawns. To keep the cookbook vegetarian, we have substituted silken tofu in this favorite recipe by the women of the collective. It has a texture that resembles fish and seafood, and the tofu absorbs the flavors. This dish is delicious and filling with rice.

Ingredients

1 Tbsp/ 15 ml cumin seeds

2 Tbsp/ 30 ml coriander seeds

½ tsp/ 2.5 ml dry red chili peppers

½ tsp/ 2.5 ml turmeric powder

1 package silken tofu

salt to taste

2 medium onions, diced

¾ cup/ 180 ml grated coconut, preferably fresh

1 tsp/ 5 ml black peppercorns

3 Tbsp/ 45 ml oil

1 medium tomato (or 10-12 cherry tomatoes), chopped

1 tsp/ 5 ml tamarind pulp

2 cups/ ½ liter of water

Method

1. In a small frying pan, lightly roast cumin seeds, coriander seeds, and dry chili peppers for 4-5 minutes over a low flame. Then grind them to powder along with turmeric.

2. Slice or dice silken tofu into cubes or strips. Add the spice mixture to the tofu, and add salt to taste and set aside.

3. In a food processor or blender, grind onion, coconut, and peppercorns into paste.

4. Heat oil in a pot. Add onions and sauté until slightly brown. Add tomatoes and tamarind and sauté again.

5. Add the onion paste and 2 cups of water to the pot. Bring to a boil.

6. Add tofu pieces and cook on a medium heat for 10-12 minutes.

Serve with hot rice or chapattis

4-6 servings   coconut   20 min   10 min

Vegan seitan "lamb" curry

by Ragini Godbole

Some Maharashtrians enjoy lamb or mutton, while others prefer to remain vegetarian. Here, we replaced the lamb with seitan, a gluten-based ingredient that has the texture and consistency of red meat. This recipe also calls for couscous, a wheat-based grain, which makes the dish warm and filling.

Ingredients

½ cup/ 120 ml couscous

2 tsp/ 10 ml salt

1 cup/ 240 ml boiling water

3 Tbsp/ 45 ml (split) oil

½ cup/ 120 ml grated coconut (preferably fresh)

1 Tbsp/ 15 ml jeera (cumin seeds)

1 Tbsp/ 15 ml sesame seeds

1 Tbsp/ 15 ml coriander seeds

2 Tbsp/ 30 ml ginger-garlic paste, or 2 cloves of garlic and one inch of ginger, minced

16 oz/ 500 gr seitan, chopped into cubes or strips

2 large red onions, chopped

1 tsp/ 5 ml salt

1 Tbsp/ 15 ml turmeric

1 tsp/ 5 ml red chili powder

Method

1. In a small, heat-resistant bowl, mix the couscous and salt, and pour boiling water over it. Cover and let the water soak up the grains.

2. In a frying pan, heat 1 tablespoon oil over medium heat. Roast the coconut, jeera, sesame seeds, coriander seeds, and ginger-garlic paste. Cook in oil for 5 minutes.

3. Place the spice mixture into a blender, food processor or grinder. Grind into a fine paste. Add a bit more oil or water to adjust the texture if necessary. Set aside.

4. In a frying pan or kadai, heat 1 tablespoon oil. Add the seitan, and fry until cooked, around 5-7 minutes. Set aside.

5. Heat 1 tablespoon of oil in the frying pan. Add onions, salt, turmeric, red chili powder, and some water. Fry until onions are soft.

6. Add the seitan, the paste, and the couscous to the frying pan. Cook for 5-10 minutes until everything is well-blended and soft.

Serve as a main dish alongside vegetables.

 4 servings
  coconut, sesame
 10 min
 30 min
 grinder or blender

mains

chinese pulav

Rice, Vegetable, and "Chicken" Pilaf
by Usha Pimpre

Pulav, a variation on the word "pilaf", is full of bright vegetables along with cubed chicken in its original version. In this recipe, the chicken has been replaced with soya beans, also known as TVP, an easy and cheap vegetarian alternative to meat.

Ingredients

- **2 cups/ ½ liter** of dried texturized vegetable protein (TVP)
- **3 Tbsp/ 45 ml** oil
- **2 medium** chili peppers, finely chopped
- **1 tsp/ 5 ml** dried chili peppers
- **1 tsp/ 5 ml** turmeric
- **1 tsp/ 5 ml** cumin
- **1 tsp/ 5 ml** ginger, grated
- **¼ cup/ 60 ml** chopped coriander leaves
- **¼ cup/ 60 ml** dill leaves, chopped
- **2 tsp/ 10 ml** salt
- **1** onion, diced
- **10** button mushrooms, sliced
- **2** carrots, diced
- **1 cup/ 240 ml** green peas
- **1 medium** head of broccoli, chopped
- **1 medium** head of cauliflower, chopped
- **2 Tbsp/ 30 ml** soy sauce
- **2 Tbsp/ 30 ml** red chili sauce
- **2 cups/ 400 gr** basmati rice
- **4 cups/ 1 liter** of water
- salt to taste
- parsley or coriander leaves for garnish
- yogurt or raita for topping

Method

1. Prepare the TVP by soaking it in a large bowl or pot of boiling water for 10-15 minutes. Next drain, rinse and squeeze out excess water. Set aside. (You can chop the vegetables during this process.)

2. Heat oil in a large, heavy pot. Add herbs – fresh and dried chili peppers, turmeric, cumin, ginger, cilantro, dill – and salt, and cook for 3-4 minutes.

3. Add onions and sauté for several minutes. Then add the rest of the chopped vegetables – mushrooms, carrots, green peas, broccoli and cauliflower – and stir fry. Add soy sauce and red chili sauce to the mix and sauté for 4-5 minutes until vegetables become slightly tender.

4. Add the TVP and stir well for 3-4 minutes making sure it soaks up the spices well.

5. Add the rice, along with 4 cups of water. Mix well and make sure the rice is covered with water. You may also want to add more salt at this point, according to your taste. Cover, bring to a boil, and simmer until the water is all soaked up. This should take around 10-15 minutes.

6. Serve hot. Garnish with chopped parsley or cilantro. You can also serve with a dollop of yogurt or raita.

4-6 servings   15 min   25 min

mains

tofu "fish" masala

by Ragini Godbole

Mumbai, surrounded on three sides by water, is a fish-loving city. Still, many of the women are vegetarian – some women eat meat once a month, some once a week, and many not at all. Several women, however, like Ragini, enjoy fish, seafood, and lamb. In this recipe, we replaced fish fillets with silken tofu. It is white, smooth and crumbly like fish, and absorbs many flavors well. It is best to let the tofu marinate in spices before cooking.

Ingredients

- **1 package** silken tofu
- **1 Tbsp/ 15 ml** turmeric
- **2 tsp/ 10 ml** red chili powder
- **1 tsp/ 5 ml** garam masala
- **1 tsp/ 5 ml** coriander
- **1 tsp/ 5 ml** salt (for marinade)
- **1 Tbsp/ 15 ml** oil (for marinade)
- **1 Tbsp/ 15 ml** oil (for frying)
- **2** onions, diced
- **2 cloves** garlic, minced
- **pinch** of salt (for sauté)
- **1 cup/ 240 ml** diced vegetables, such as mushrooms, zucchinis, carrots, or broccoli (optional)
- **1/2 cup/ 120 ml** grated coconut, preferably fresh

Method

1. Dice the tofu into cubes or strips, or crumble into small pieces (silken tofu has a tendency to crumble). Place in a flat dish to marinate. In a small bowl, whisk together the turmeric, chili powder, garam masala, coriander, and salt along with the oil and a bit of water. Pour over the tofu, coating it well. Let it marinade for 15-20 minutes.

2. Heat oil in a large frying pan or kadai over high heat. Add onions, garlic, and a pinch of salt, and cook until they are translucent, around 4-5 minutes. If you would like to add your choice of vegetables to this dish, sauté them for 5 minutes.

3. Add tofu, and stir-fry over a medium flame; the tofu will crumble into the mixture.

4. Add a tablespoon of water if necessary so that the tofu does not burn. Continue cooking for 10 minutes or until the tofu has absorbed the flavors, stirring regularly. Add coconut and stir for one more minute.

Serve with chapattis or rotis, or over rice or couscous.

4 servings — coconut, soy — 20 min — 15 min

Sweets are enjoyed not only during meals but also at tea-time and as snacks. They are also used for the prasad, the offering, in many festival pujahs or rituals. The gods like the snacks as much as the women do.

SWEETS

Galub Jamun
Badam Halwa
Steamed Modak
Sweet Kachori
Nariyal Barfi
Basundi
Apple Kheer
Gajar Halwa
Baluhashi
Safarshand Barfi
Shankarpali
Moong Dahl Halwa

Yield: 100

The women have a unique daily challenge of cooking healthy, delicious food for hundreds of schoolchildren at a time, who are studying at the GPM Love2Learn school in Kalwa. This task requires special love and attention – and massive quantities of food. Here is an example of a "Yield:100" recipe. It is Soya Bean Pulav, a combination of rice and soya chunks also known as TVP, a cheap vegetarian alternative to chicken. They are high in protein and easy to prepare. Except for the part where they have to purchase huge sacks of equipment, which usually gets transported through the slum alleys on the women's heads. Their impressive neck muscles are matched only by the arm strength required for stirring the massive pots. More power to the women – literally.

Soya Bean Pulav for 100

Yield: 100 children's portions

Ingredients

13 lbs/ 6 kgs rice
1 lb/ ½ kg masoor dal (flat orange lentils)
2 lbs/ 1 kg soyabean chunks
2 lbs/ 1 kg oil
2 lbs/ 1 kg onions, sliced
½ lb/ ¼ kg garlic, chopped
2-3 tsp/ 10-15 ml salt
⅓ cup/ 30 gr jeera (cumin seeds)
¼ cup/ 20 gr haldi (turmeric powder)
¼ cup/ 20 gr garam masala
½ cup/ 60 gr onion and garlic masala
handful of kothimbir (cilantro)
8-10 bay leaves
8-10 strands of curry leaves
1 lb/ ½ kg green peas
1 lb/ ½ kg tomatoes, chopped
2 lbs/ 1 kg potatoes, diced

Method

1. Rinse rice and soak for 30 minutes in water. Rinse and soak dal for 30 minutes in water.
2. Soak soya bean chunks for 15 minutes in water. The beans will absorb water and double in size. Drain the excess water and rinse.
3. Heat oil in large pot. Add onion, garlic, salt and jeera, and stir as it fries for 2-3 minutes. Then add the turmeric, masalas, coriander, bay leaves and curry leaves and stir together well, until the onion turns transparent.
4. Add peas, tomatoes and potatoes, and stir well, coating the vegetables in the onion-spice mixture. Let it cook for 5-7 minutes, until softened.
5. Add the rice along with water in a 2:1 ratio (1 kg of rice is 5 cups, which would mean that 6 kgs of rice require 60 cups or roughly 4 gallons or 16 liters of water).
6. Add the dal, along with similar ratios of water (½ kg of dal takes 5 cups or 1 ¼ liters of water).
7. Stir really well. (Perhaps go to the gym first.)
8. Cover and bring to a boil. Let simmer on a low flame for 5-10 minutes.
9. Drain the soya chunks once more and add to the pot. Stir well. (Again.)
10. Cook until the water is soaked up, and the rice and dal are fully cooked, around 5 more minutes. Pour into 100 small tiffens for the children. Serve hot (but not too hot!)

gulab jamun

"Rose Berry" Milky Dessert Balls
by Jayshree Kondwal

One of the most popular desserts in India, these sweet, sticky, puffy balls require a few hours of waiting during the preparation. The milk-base pistachios blend, covered in the coating of cardamom and rose water gives this dish a distinct, very sweet milky flavor. They can be served warm or at room temperature.

Ingredients

- **½ cup/ 64 gr** all-purpose flour
- **1 cup/ 128 gr** milk powder (khoya)
- **1 pinch** baking soda
- **1 tsp/ 5 ml** oil or ghee
- **1 Tbsp/ 15 ml** yogurt
- **1 Tbsp/ 15 ml** milk
- oil for frying

For sugar syrup:

- **1 cup/ 237 ml** water
- **1 cup/ 237 ml** sugar
- **4** green cardamom pods
- **few drops** of rose water
- **1 tsp/ 5 ml** chopped pistachios for garnish

Method

1. Mix together flour, milk powder and baking soda. Add ghee, yogurt and milk. Mix well to form a dough. Grease your palms if sticky.

2. Divide the dough into 12-14 golf ball-sized balls. Heat oil in a frying pan over medium heat. Put the balls in the pan and fry till golden brown, around 5 minutes on each side.

3. Meanwhile, create the sugar syrup by mixing together water, sugar and crushed cardamom in a small saucepan over medium to high heat. Bring to a boil and then lower the flame. Stir with a wooden spoon until the syrup turns slightly sticky. Simmer on a very low flame while the galub jamun balls are frying.

4. After the balls are done, drain in a colander. Then dip each ball into the syrup.

5. Allow to rest for 3 hours, till the balls absorb the syrup and puff up.

Garnish with pistachios and serve, warm or room temperature.

8-10 servings · pistachios · 10 min · 30 min

badam halwa
Almond Pudding
by Hirabai Vilas Umbarkar

The almond pudding is one of the most popular and famous Indian desserts, a favorite among children and nostalgic for adults alike. It is also very high in protein and is often suggested for pregnant women who crave sweets. The recipe calls for peeled almonds, which requires a tedious task of hand-peeling soaked almonds. Doing this process alone makes you appreciate the significance of group cooking. When the women of the collective sit around peeling mountains of almonds, they talk, laugh, and enjoy being together while getting the job done quickly! It is no wonder that they shared missing this part of their village lives after they left and before they began working together in rebuilding that culture.

Ingredients

1 cup/ 150 gr almonds (badam)

2 cups/ ½ liter water or milk

1 cup/ 180 gr sugar

¼ cup/ 60 ml ghee or coconut oil

½ tsp/ 7.5 ml cardamom powder

5-6 drops of rose water (optional)

5-6 slivers of saffron (optional)

almond slivers for garnish

Method

1. Combine the almonds and enough water in a deep bowl and soak for 6-7 hours.

2. Drain the almonds, and remove the skin from each almond.

3. Blend the skinned almonds in a blender until you get a coarse mixture. Be careful not make it too thin, trying to retain a slightly coarse texture.

4. Heat the ghee or oil in a non-stick frying pan or kadhai. Add the almond mixture and then the sugar. Bring to a boil while stirring constantly. Once it has boiled, lower the flame a bit, but most importantly, continue stirring to make sure that it does not burn at the bottom. Note that the boiling process will make the mixture splatter a bit so best to keep some distance from the pan.

5. After around 10-15 minutes, when the boiling process settles down and the mixture begins to thicken, add more ghee or oil, along with cardamom, rose water and saffron (optional). Continue stirring for another 10-15 minutes until the mixture begins to separate from the sides of the pan.

Serve warm and garnished with cardamom powder or almond slivers.

sweets

 4-6 servings

 almonds

 1 hour
 30 min
 6-7 hours overnight soaking
 blender

Steamed Modak

by Jayshree Chavdry

Modaks, sweet dumplings with a distinctive sun-like shape, are an essential part of the pujah of the Ganesh Chaturthi, a 10-day festival in August or September that celebrates Ganesh, the elephant-head god. The festival is marked not only by chants and fasts, but also by offerings of "prasad", trays of treats. Modaks are believed to be a Ganesh favorite, and the women of the collective spend weeks preparing for the festival – not only for the god, but also for the community to enjoy. Modaks come in a variety of flavors. This variation is stuffed with a raisin/sultana mixture.

Ingredients

For stuffing (saran):

2 Tbsp/ 30 ml oil or ghee

2 cups/ ½ liter ground fresh coconut

2 cup/ ½ liter jaggery

1 ½ tsp/ 12.5 ml cardamom

1 cup/ 240 ml raisins or sultanas

For outer cover:

2 cups/ 256 gr all-purpose flour

salt to taste

¾ cup/ 177 ml water

2 tsp/ 10 ml oil

Method

1. In a large frying pan, heat a tsp of clarified butter or ghee on a medium to low flame. Add ground coconut and keep stirring constantly to avoid sticking at the bottom.

2. When the coconut becomes light brown, after around 3-4 minutes, add jaggery. Allow jaggery to melt, stirring constantly, for 2-3 minutes.

3. Add cardamom powder and mix well. Add raisins and coat with the spice mixture. The modakache saran (stuffing) is ready. Set aside.

4. While the saran is cooling down, make the dough for the outer cover. In a mixing bowl, combine 2 cups of sifted wheat flour and salt. Begin kneading the dough as you gradually add water. Dough should be soft and pliable. Add oil and knead again. Cover and let rest for 15-20 minutes.

5. When the dough is ready, make small balls, about the size of a large cherry tomato.

6. Grease a steamer, where you will place the modaks after assembly. Meanwhile, pour a few centimeters of water into a big pot and let the water begin to heat up as you prepare the modaks.

7. To assemble the modaks, take one ball, dip into flour, and roll it like a small puri (flat disk). It should not be very thin or very thick, ideally a few millimeters thick. Place a spoonful of stuffing on it in the middle. Then, fold the edges so that you get the shape of a modak. It should look like flames of the sun coming out from the disk. When you have the desired shape, close the top and

8-10 modaks coconut 40 min 20 min

give it a point, like a chocolate Hershey's kiss. Place it into the greased steamer. Follow the same procedure to make the rest of the modaks and assemble carefully in the steamer.

8. Your water should be boiled by now, and steam should be coming out of it. Now place the steamer with the modaks on top of the pot and cover it. Allow modaks to steam for around 10 minutes.

Serve in the "prasad" (the tray used in the Pujah ceremony) for Ganesh, or prepare for yourself and your family and community! Enjoy!

Sweet Kachori

Stuffed Sweet Dough
by Manisha Sable

This Maharashtrian sweet dough stuffed with dried fruits and nuts is a favorite dessert for the women of the collective and a great way to get kids to enjoy healthy dried fruit. It can be made with or without the sugar syrup coating. Kachoris can be stored in an airtight container and stay for several days.

Ingredients

For the dough:

1 cup/ 128 gr all-purpose flour

½ tsp/ 2.5 ml salt

1 Tbsp/ 15 ml ghee

½ cup/ 120 ml fresh cream

For the filling:

½ cup/ 75 gr dried fruits, nuts, or raisins, diced

¼ cup/ 25 gr ground coconut flakes

½ cup/ 100 gr khoya (powdered milk)

½ cup/ 100 gr powdered sugar

oil for deep frying

For syrup coating (optional):

1 cup/ 200 gr sugar

1 cup/ 237 ml water

Method

1. In a large mixing bowl combine flour and salt. Add the ghee and mix with your hands until you get a crumbly texture. Add the cream and mix together with a spoon until you get a nice, soft dough. You may need to add a bit of water, but the dough should be firm and not liquidy. Once the cream is incorporated, knead for a few minutes until the dough has a consistent texture. Set aside.

2. In another bowl, combine the fruit and nuts with khoya, coconut, and powdered sugar. Set aside.

3. Take the dough and roll it into a long roll, around 3 inches (7-8 cm) in diameter. Slice the roll into discs, around 1 inch thick (2.5 cm).

4. Take a disc and flatten it. Take a teaspoon of the filling and place it in the center of the disc. Fold the dough around the filling and seal it on top. Dab a bit of water onto the top to keep it sealed well. You should have roughly a ball shape. Now, flatten it a bit more. Make sure no filling is sticking out. If you have to seal up a hole, use a bit of water to bring the dough together. Repeat this step for all the discs and have around 8-10 pieces.

5. Heat oil in a deep saucepan or wok over medium heat. Insert the pieces into the hot oil, and lower the heat. It is important for the kachoris to fry slowly in order for the dough to be fully cooked inside. It will take around 8-10 minutes per batch.

6. If you would like a sugary syrup coating, then make the syrup while the kachoris are frying. In a small saucepan, combine sugar and water and bring to a boil, stirring occasionally until the sugar is absorbed and the liquid is a bit sticky.

8-10 units   almonds, coconut   15 min   20 min

7. When the kachoris are nice and crispy on the outside, drain them in a colander. For sugar coating, dip the kachoris into the sugar syrup and let them set.

Garnish with almonds or coconut. These can stay fresh for 2-3 days in an airtight container.

When Hirabai was growing up in the village of Mahabaleshwar in the Satara district of Maharashtra, India, there was no school nearby. The children would go to the temple, and the man who was in charge of caring for the temple would sit them down and tell them things, whatever he knew to tell them. He was the closest thing she knew to having a teacher. And this is what they would call school. Around the time she would have been in the third grade, the man stopped doing that, and that was the end of her education.

When Hirabai was 15 years old, she got married and moved to Mumbai. There were many things she missed about her village. She has memories of plucking strawberries while she played with her friends. She misses being close to the land and working the fields with her extended family. Even though it was hot in the fields, she loved the experience of being at work with her whole family.

She also misses her friends. Like any 15-year-old girl who suddenly moved from home, she is sad about losing those important connections. She says that almost all her friends have left the village, and none live close by. Hirabai naturally made new friends in Kalwa. "The women in the collective are dear friends," she says. "We talk and share recipes. The group is very important to me."

Today, Hirabai is 43 years old and lives in Kalwa with her husband and their three children. The oldest daughter, 26, is married. The second daughter, 22, works for a hi-tech company in Mumbai. The youngest boy is in college. Over the next few years, after all her children are on their own, she plans to move back to the village. She hopes her son will come too.

Hirabai's favorite foods are the faral foods that are made for Diwali, although she also makes it during the year, too. Faral is actually is a combination of lots of sweet things. Her recipe for shankarpali is included in this book, along with a whole series of sweets: badam halwa, modaks, basundi, coconut barfi, and apple kheer. She serves the faral for tea-time or for a snack. But there is a special experience of exchanging the sweet snacks along with sweet blessings for one another.

hirabai vilas umbarkar

nariyal barfi

Coconut Confectionary
by Hirabai Vilas Umbarkar

This sweet coconut dessert is quick and simple to make, and has only a few ingredients. Working with the coconut-sugar combination requires some attention, so do not walk away from the pan while you are making this! Once you get the method, this will become an easy, go-to dessert when you need a quick dish or have unexpected visitors.

Ingredients

2 Tbsp/ 30 ml ghee, divided

2 cups/ 200 gr grated coconut

1 cup/ 200 gr sugar

1 tsp/ 5 ml cardamom powder

almonds or pistachios for garnish

Method

1. Heat a large frying pan over a medium heat. Heat 1 Tbsp ghee. Add coconut and cook for a minute. Keep stirring to avoid burning.

2. Add sugar and stir, continuing cooking over a medium heat. Add cardamom powder. Mixture will start thickening in 7-8 minutes.

3. Grease a glass dish or baking pan with 1 Tbsp of ghee and spread the mixture evenly around 1 cm-thick. After 2-3 minutes, use a knife lightly cut through 2-inch pieces, but do not separate them.

4. After the mixture is fully cooled, separate the pieces. Garnish with almonds or pistachios while it is still hot.

10-12 servings | | | | coconuts, almonds/ pistachios | 2 min | 10 min | |

basundi

Milk Pudding
by Hirabai Vilas Umbarkar

The original version of this milk-based pudding calls for creating condensed milk from scratch by simmering and stirring a liter of whole milk for an hour and thus reducing it by half. Or if you prefer, you can purchase canned condensed milk and mix it with a cup of whole milk, simmering together for ten minutes.

Ingredients

2 cups/ ½ liter condensed milk

1 cup/ 237 ml whole milk

½ cup/ 100 gr white sugar

1 tsp/ 5 ml ground cardamom

½ tsp/ 2.5 ml ground nutmeg or whole nutmeg for grating

2 Tbsp/ 30 ml unsalted almonds, chopped

2 Tbsp/ 30 ml unsalted cashews, chopped

2 Tbsp/ 30 ml shelled pistachios, chopped

raisins, dried fruit, or dried nuts for garnish

Method

1. In a heavy-bottomed pan, mix together the condensed milk and regular milk and bring to a boil. As it starts boiling, reduce the heat to medium.

2. Add sugar, cardamom and nutmeg, and keep stirring for 10 minutes. Mix well so that the texture is not grainy.

3. Add chopped almonds, cashews, pistachios. Mix well and let simmer for 5 more minutes. The mixture should be thick yet also runny.

4. Refrigerate overnight or until chilled, and serve in small bowls with dried fruit.

4-6 servings | 2 min | 15 min

sweets

apple kheer

Apple Pudding
by Hirabai Vilas Umbarkar

This sweet and healthy creamy apple pudding dessert that is especially satisfying in the winter months and among children.

Ingredients

4 cups/ 1 liter condensed milk

1 cup/ 237 ml whole milk

2 Tbsp/ 30 ml ghee or butter

2 medium apples, peeled and grated

½ cup/ 100 gr of sugar

1 Tbsp/ 15 ml of green cardamom powder

1 tsp/ 5 ml cinnamon powder

½ cup/ 75 gr chopped cashews, almonds, and/or pistachios

Method

1. Bring the milk and condensed milk to a boil in a large, thick-bottom pan over medium to low heat and simmer until it thickens. Stir occasionally to keep it from burning on the bottom.

2. Meanwhile, heat ghee or butter in a frying pan. Add the apple mixture and cook on medium heat. Add sugar and stew until the sugar melts. Continue to cook until most of the moisture evaporates, around 10-15 minutes. Add sugar, cardamom and cinnamon, and cook for 2-3 more minutes, until the sugar is fully dissolved.

3. Add the apple mixture to the milk and stir well for 2-3 minutes. Turn off the heat, and add the nuts and blend well. You may opt to run the mixture through a blender for a creamier texture.

Place the pudding into small bowls and chill in the refrigerator for 2-3 hours. Serve chilled, garnished with almonds or cashews.

4-6 servings | cashews, almonds, pistachios | 10 min | 30 min

gajar halwa

Carrot Pudding
by Indu Sona Mane

This bright, colorful pudding uses carrots as a dessert. The blend of nuts, cardamom and sugar create a light, sweet flavor, and a Maharashtrian favorite. This is the dish that Indu is presenting to her western guests with pride and joy on the cover of this cookbook.

Ingredients

- **3 Tbsp/ 45 ml** ghee or coconut oil
- **2 lbs/ 1 kg** carrots, grated
- **¼ cup/ 50 gr** powdered milk (khoya/mawa)
- **1 Tbsp/ 15 ml** cardamom powder (or 8-10 crushed green cardamom pods)
- **¼ cup/ 50 gr** cashews, crushed
- **¼ cup/ 50 gr** almonds, crushed
- **2 cups/ 400 gr** sugar (optional)
- **½ cup/ 120 ml** whole milk (optional)

Method

1. Rinse, peel and grate the carrots.

2. Heat ghee or oil in a large non-stick frying pan or kadai. Add the grated carrots. Sauté over medium heat until the carrots turn tender and are cooked. Keep stirring in intervals while sautéing the carrots, around 15-20 minutes.

3. Add the khoya and stir until it is blended, around 4-5 minutes.

4. Add cardamom powder, cashews and almonds. Stir again and simmer on a low flame. Be sure to stir often until the mixture dries up and reduces, around 10 more minutes. You may add sugar and milk as an option and continue to simmer and mix until it is all blended and soft.

Gajar Halwa can be served either, hot, warm or cold. Garnish with nuts.

sweets

 4 servings

 almonds, cashews
 10 min
 30 min

balushahi

Sweet Dumplings
by Alka Harishchandra Gaikwad

This popular snack of fried dough covered in sweet syrup makes a great accompaniment to tea any time of the day. The recipe is straightforward, but getting the texture of the dough just right so it fries correctly and retains its special shape can take some practice. According to the women of the collective, the effort is worth it. Alka recommends making a big batch so you can grab a balushahi along with a cup of chai whenever you get the craving!

Ingredients

For the balls:

2 ½ cups/ 320 gr all-purpose flour (maida)

1 tsp/ 5 ml baking soda

¼ cup/ 60 ml yogurt or paneer

¾ cup/ 177 ml warm water

¾ cup/ 177 ml ghee or oil for the mixture

oil or ghee for deep frying

For the sugar syrup:

½ cup/ 100 gr sugar

1 cup/ 237 ml water

For the frying:

ghee for frying

crushed nuts for garnish

Method

1. Prepare the dough: Place flour and baking soda into a large mixing bowl. Add yogurt and water and knead well. The dough should be soft. Add flour or water if the proportions need adjustment. Set aside and let the dough rest for 15-20 minutes.

2. Meanwhile, begin to prepare the sugar syrup. Place the water and sugar into a small saucepan and heat over a low flame until the sugar is all absorbed.

3. Fry the balls. Separate the dough into golf ball-sized pieces. Flatten them a bit, and press your thumb into the center of the ball. Meanwhile, heat oil in a wok or deep pot. When the oil is hot, lower the flame and insert balushahis into the oil. It should fry slowly so the insides are fully cooked through and through. When they are ready, after around ten minutes, they will "pop up" to the top of the pot. Turn them over to make sure they are browned on both sides. When they are ready, take them out and place them on a paper towel, towel, or colander to drain the excess oil.

4. To drench the balls with sugar syrup, hold each ball in a spoon with one hand while you pour the syrup onto each ball.

Garnish with crushed nuts in the thumbprint and your balushahi is ready. Store them in an air-tight container for up to 15 days and eat whenever you crave this extraordinarily delicious dessert.

yields 15-20 pieces

nuts

40 min

20 min

sweets

Mangal Vittal Mane

Mangal, a 48-year-old mother of two from the Takali village near Pune, Maharashtra, lost her husband of thirty years just three years ago. He died suddenly at the age of 51 from a heart attack, making Mangal the only woman in the collective who is no longer living with her husband. As she tells this story to me and the women of the collective, the women around her sigh. Their sadness, as well as their friendship and care, are palpable.

Mangal was married at the age of fifteen, and stayed in school through the fifth grade. She and her late husband moved to Kalwa 28 years ago, one of the earliest arrivals in the group. He was working in a government job, so they had a certain degree of financial stability.

Still, Mangal continues to miss her village even though she has been in Kalwa for so many years. Her village of Takali has land and fields, and people come together many times a year to harvest, even though it is hard and what she refers to as "sweaty work." She tells me that what she misses about her village is the coming together of her entire family.

She, like all the women in the group, also loves the festivals at her village and she takes every opportunity to return home. "Every time you mention villages to the women", she says, "their faces light up. Everyone misses the villages." What is so apparent to me is that though many of the women like Mangal have lived in Mumbai for many years, the villages that they left remain a focal point in their lives.

Working in the women's cooperative marks the first time in Mangal's life that she has ever worked out of the home, and Mangal likes that. "I am often alone," she says, since her husband is gone and her children are grown. Her 27-year-old son works in the railway and her 23-year-old is a pharmacist. "Getting together with the women is very nice for me. Plus, I earn some money. Mostly, I love being with the women."

Ultimately, Mangal dreams of her children getting married and finding homes of their own. Once the children are settled, she plans to return to her village. "I came here for my children," she says, "to help them build a life for themselves. Once that is done, I can go back home." Having thought very carefully about this, she tells me that she plans to go back to her village and work in the fields herself rather than hiring others. She no longer wants to be dependent on anyone to help her. It is clear that the women's collective has facilitated her independence even in the midst of her tragedy. She is going to do it on her own.

Mangal contributed paneer masala, paneer parathi, savory appe, and safarchand barfi to this cookbook, which are some of her favorite dishes.

safarchand barfi

Apple Bars
by Mangal Vittal Mane

Apples are a common base for desserts among the women. This barfi, or a pan of flat, square bars, offers an interesting take on western dessert bars. Here, it is best to use sweet apples with bright red skin, such as pink lady or macintosh varieties, rather than sour apples. This recipe uses unpeeled apples that are dried into a paste by frying. The aroma of apples in ghee or butter is phenomenal, and worth the time and patience to get the right consistency. The result is sweet and delicious.

Ingredients

4 medium apples, grated

juice of one lemon

1 Tbsp/ 15 ml ghee or butter

½ cup/ 120 ml apple juice

½ cup/ 100 gr sugar

½ cup/ 100 gr condensed milk powder (khoya)

2 tsp/ 10 ml powdered cinnamon

½ cup/ 60 gr of chopped almonds, cashews and/or pistachios

Method

1. In a mixing bowl, combine grated apples and lemon juice. Then, squeeze the excess liquid out of the mixture.

2. In a large frying pan or kadai, heat ghee or butter on a high heat. Add apples and sauté, mixing occasionally to make sure it does not stick.

3. Add apple juice and sugar to the pan and mix well. When the sugar dissolves, and the mixture thickens, add khoya and cook, stirring continuously for 10-15 minutes, until the mixture is dry and firm.

4. Meanwhile grease a tray with ghee. Sprinkle the chopped almonds, cashew nuts and pistachios on it.

5. When the apple mixture begins to leave the sides of the pan, transfer onto the tray. Refrigerate for a few hours to set.

Once the barfi is set, cut into pieces and serve.

sweets

 8-10 servings   almonds, nuts, pistachios 15 min 30 min

Shankarpali

Sweet Biscuits
by Hirabai Vilas Umbarkar

The women love Diwali, the annual festival of lights that takes place in the autumn. They have memories of making "faral", special sweets for Diwali that they exchange with each other as a gesture of friendship and festivity. Indu says that the women in her family would spend weeks together preparing the faral. Hirabai says that the Shankarpali, these sweet diamond-shaped biscuits, are a favorite of hers not only for Diwali but also all year round.

Ingredients

½ cup/ 120 ml ghee or butter

½ cup/ 120 ml milk

½ cup/ 100 gr white sugar

2 ½ cups/ 320 gr all-purpose flour

1 tsp/ 5 ml semolina flour

1 tsp/ 5 ml salt

oil for deep frying

Method

1. In a small saucepan, mix the ghee and the milk. Bring to a quick boil and shut off the heat.

2. Add sugar and stir well.

3. Pour the mixture into a large mixing bowl. Add the flour, semolina and salt, and knead well for 5-10 minutes, until the dough is smooth and firm. Let it rest for 30 minutes.

4. Roll out the dough into a flat sheet, not too thin. It should be around a centimeter or half an inch in thickness, or even a bit thicker.

5. Using a sharp knife or pizza knife, cut the sheet into a grid so that the pieces are all diamond shape.

6. Heat the oil in a wok, kadai, or deep pot, over medium to high heat. Carefully place the pieces into the hot oil and deep fry until all sides are brown, around 5-7 minutes. Do not fry on the highest heat because then the insides may not be fully cooked. Slower is better.

7. When they are done, drain them on a towel or in a colander.

Store in an airtight container or bag. The biscuits can serve as a delicious sweet for the entire Diwali festival.

Enjoy!!

> **TIP:** For a delicious cinnamon flavor, add a tablespoon of powdered cinnamon with the flour before you knead the dough.

15-20 biscuits | 10 min | 20 min | 30 min dough rise

sweets

moong dahl halwa

Lentil Pudding
By Sangita Raut

This halwa dessert on a base of yellow or orange lentils has the consistency of sweet semolina, but is much higher in protein and nutrients. It is very sweet with a distinct Maharashtrian twinge of cardamom and saffron.

Ingredients

2 cups/ 360 gr moong dal

1 cup/ 200 gr sugar

2 cups/ ½ liter whole milk

1 ½ cups/ 360 ml ghee

1 Tbsp/ 15 ml cardamom powder

5-6 strands of saffron (optional)

¼ cup/ 30 gr crushed almonds

Method

1. Soak moong dal in a bowl of water for 2-3 hours. After it is soaked, drain and rinse.

2. In an electric blender or food processor, puree the lentils with sugar and milk. The paste should be thick, coarse and heavy.

3. In a large non-stick frying pan or kadai, heat the ghee on a medium flame. Pour the paste into the ghee, and let it cook, stirring constantly with a strong, heavy serving spoon or wooden spoon. Make sure to get all the lumps out. Add a bit more milk and lower the flame if the bottom begins to burn. Continue to cook and stir the mixture for 20-30 minutes, until the color has faded and the aroma of raw lentils has gone. The mixture should be lump-free but a bit coarse.

4. Add cardamom, saffron and almonds and mix together for 2-3 minutes.

Garnish with almonds or cardamom powder.

 6-8 servings   almonds 5 min 35 min 2-3 hour soak blender

जयश्री रविंद्र केंडवळ

✳ म्हैसूर भजी ✳

साहित्य :- १ वाटी मैदा, १ वाटी दही (आंबट असल्यास उत्तम) मैद्याच्या १/५ भाग इतका रवा, ४ चमचे साखर, मीठ, अर्धा चमचा बेकिंग सोडा, जिरे, किसलेले ओले खोबरे, हिरवी मिरची, कोथिंबीर बारीक चिरलेली.

कृती :- एका पातेल्यात मैदा घेऊन त्यात जिरे, मीठ, साखर, सोडा, खोबरे हिरवी मिरची कोथिंबीर, रवा हे सगळे जिन्नस व्यवस्थित मिसळून घ्यावे. गरजेनुसार त्यात दही मिसळावे ते हलक्या हाताने एकजीव करावे. नंतर ते पीठ १ ते २ तास आंबवून घ्यावे. एका कढईत तेल गरम करून नंतर त्या पीठाचे मध्यम आकाराचे गोळे बनवून ते मध्यम आचेवर तेलात तळून घ्यावे. म्हैसूर भजी तयार कोणत्याही चटणीसोबत सर्व्ह करावे.

✳ गुलाब जामुन ✳

(गुलाब जामुनसाठी)

साहित्य :- दूध, खवा, वाटी, साखर, तेल किंवा तूप, गिट्स गुलाब जामुनचे पॅकेट, वेलची, केसर

कृती :- स्वादिष्ट गुलाब जामुन बनविण्यासाठी २५०-३०० मिली पाणी खव्यामिक्स मध्ये घेऊन चांगले मिसळून

index of the women's recipes

Alka Harishchandra Gaikwad   profile p. 100
- anda masala (egg stew), 52
- balushahi (sweet dumplings), 196
- curd kadhi (yogurt stew), 98
- maswadi (gram flour fritters), 118
- tikhat bakri (spicy wheat flatbread), 72

Hirabai Vilas Umbarkar   profile p. 190
- apple kheer (apple pudding), 194
- badam halwa (almond pudding), 185
- basundi (sweet snacks), 192
- bharwa bindi (stuffed "lady fingers", okra), 131
- nariyal barfi (coconut confectionary), 191

Indu Sona Mane   profile p. 54
- cardamom lassi (yogurt drink), 56
- gajar halwa (carrot pudding), 195
- kokum sharbat (kokum fruit drink), 57
- kolhapur vegetable masala, 162
- methi poori (fenugreek crispbread), 68
- pav bhaji (stew served on buns), 156
- puran poli (sweet stuffed flatbread), 120
- upma (savory porridge), 83

Jayshree Chavdry
- steamed modak, 186
- shepu bhaji (dill stew), 155
- tikhat poori (spicy crispbread), 76

Jayshree Kondwal
- galub jamun ("rose berry" milky dessert balls), 184
- mysore bhajji (yogurt fritters,) 122

Kalpana Gawde   profile p. 166
- aloo paratha (potato-stuffed flatbread), 80
- kala chana amti (black chickpea stew), 110
- palak paneer (spinach and white cheese stew), 167
- tomato chutney (tomato dip), 96

Kamal Shivaji Kadam   profile p. 124
- aam panha (raw mango drink), 52
- capsicum (bell pepper) potato masala, 161
- coconut-cauliflower curry, 147
- kanda bhajji (onion fritters), 125
- mango chutney (mango dip), 103
- methi samosas (fenugreek pastries), 128
- palak paratha (spinach-stuffed flatbread), 92

Mangal Vittal Mane   profile p. 198
- paneer masala (white-cheese stew), 108
- paneer paratha (cheese-stuffed flatbread), 90
- safarchand barfi (apple bars), 199
- savory appam (pancake puffs), 126

Manisha Sable   profile p. 60
- sol kadi (coconut-kokum drink), 61
- sweet kachori (stuffed sweet dough), 188

Maya Kadu   profile p. 104
- coconut chutney (coconut dip), 101
- ghavan (spicy crepes), 82
- muramba kairicha (mango preserve), 105
- potato bhaji (potato stew), 127

- rice dosas (rice-flour pancakes), 81
- vegetable biryani (rice-vegetable pilaf), 172

Ragini Godbole   profile p. 174
- "fish" tofu masala, 180
- jal jeera (cumin water), 59
- lamb curry, 176
- mango lassi (mango-yogurt drink), 53
- "seafood" tofu curry, 175

Ranjana Ramchandra Gaikwad
- chana masala (chickpea stew), 152
- classic poori (round crispbread), 66
- moong dahl (lentil stew), 160

Rohini Mahamuni
- bharli wangi (brinjal – stuffed baby eggplants), 170
- fullower batata rassa (cauliflower-potato stew), 168
- kanda poha (riceflake cereal with onion), 88
- kothimbir wadi (coriander fritters), 138

Sangita Raut   profile p. 84
- alu wadi rolls (taro leaf cutlets), 130
- besan dhirde (chickpea "omelet"), 85
- kanda lasun chutney (onion-garlic spice mix), 106
- limbu sharbat (sweet lemon juice), 56
- mattar paneer (peas and white cheese stew), 164
- moong dahl halwa (lentil pudding), 202
- sabudana wada (tapioca fritters), 86

Subhadra Khose   profile p. 140
- medu wada (lentil fritters), 136
- upvas masala idli (fasting sponge-ball snacks), 141

Usha Pimpre
- banana cutlets. 139
- Chinese pulav (rice, vegetable, and "chicken" pilaf), 178
- paneer pakoda (cheese fritters), 137
- upvas puri bhaji (potato topping for crispbread during fasts), 127
- upvas rajgira puri (amaranth crispbreads for fasting), 135

Other contributors

Hayley Dsouza   profile p. 112
Hayley Dsouza is the Educational Coordinator of Gabriel Project Mumbai and Thane resident. She worked as a translator and cultural mediator for the cookbook.
- mango pickle, 113
- chili-mushroom pakora (tempura-fried mushrooms), 142

Victoria Mendes
Victoria Mendes is a veteran caterer and works as staff in the Delicio kitchen where she helps manage the process of cooking for hundreds of children every day.
- egg pulav (egg pilaf), 158

Chef Moshe Shek
Chef Moshe Shek, founder of the Moshe's restaurant chain in India, donated his time, facilities and expertise to help train the women.
- Moshe's Jeera poori (cumin crispbread), 69

Gloria Spielman
Gloria Spielman is a British-Israeli phenomenal home cook whose Bombay-born mother taught her many secrets of Indian cooking. Gloria served as an informal consultant on the cookbook.
- aloo samosas (potato- and pea-stuffed savory pastries), 132

about gabriel project mumbai

Gabriel Project Mumbai (GPM) is an NGO that works with local communities in caring for vulnerable children in slums and under-served rural villages by providing a grassroots response to poverty, malnutrition, disease, illiteracy, hunger,. and child labor in India.

Founded in 2012, GPM uses a creative, compassionate, and carefully-crafted strategic approach of The Triad of Children's Well-Being. By attending to three core issues simultaneously - education, health and nutrition - GPM creates the best environment to maximize the ability of vulnerable children to change the trajectory of their lives.

Education: Love2Learn School Network. Educational opportunity is a key factor in breaking the cycles of poverty. GPM provides formal and informal schooling to over 1000 children living in urban slums and 25 rural poor villages around Mumbai. The Love2Learn school network serves families in Kalwa, Thane, and in the remote tribal villages of Palgar District of Maharashtra. The Love2Learn educational network is built on the understanding that all children deserve access to high-quality education. Love2Learn provides an innovative, student-centered, and progressive program for every child.

Nutrition: Eat2Learn Nutrition Program. The most gripping barrier to children's growth is hunger. When families do not have food security, everything else falls by the wayside. In order to alleviate children's hunger and to prevent child labor, GPM provides a simple yet powerful solution: Eat to Learn. This signature program provides hot, nutritious meals to children learning in classes every school day. These hot meals offer children – and their parents – a wonderful incentive to stay in school rather than send children to work.

Health: The Shravan Health Center. In 2015, GPM opened the first ever medical clinic for mothers and children in the Kalwa slum, serving a community of 200,000 people. The clinic, in partnership with Doctors for You, provides a wide range of accessible services, including sick visits, vaccinations, tuberculosis treatment, medical outreach and more. The clinic also treats malnourished babies and children as part of the Dr. Gerald J. Friedman Infant Malnutrition Intervention Program. In rural villages, GPM also provides a mobile clinic to serve the medical needs of families in remote tribal areas.

Community Development

In addition to providing services for vulnerable children, GPM takes a strategic approach to community development, initiating projects that advance the health and well-being of entire communities in the slums and in remote villages. In the urban areas, this includes a safe-drinking water project, The Joshua Jacob Greenberger Learning Center, grass-roots social enterprises, and more. In the remote villages, community development includes water and agricultural projects, community centers, and improving health and education. The goal of community development is to get communities engaged, involved and empowered.

Women's Empowerment

Development is intricately tied to women's empowerment because when women thrive, entire communities thrive. GPM advances women's social enterprise and economic development to create a win-win model for social change – like the Masala Mamas project, in which women are the driving force behind nutrition, literacy and education. This model for community development enables the women to receive a powerful social and economic boost while creating ripples of change throughout the entire community.

GPM relies on partnerships with local grass-roots businesses and NGO partners, as well as friends and supporters around the world.

For more information, go to www.gabrielprojectmumbai.org,
or contact info@gabrielprojectmumbai.org.

Follow us on Facebook and Twitter: @GabrielPMumbai

our ngo partners

Humble Smile Foundation
"A healthy smile is important for physical, psychological and social development and well-being, and home-cooked meals are the key to a healthy smile! It has been a special experience working with some of India's Masala Mamas on our Gabriel Smiles oral health promotion project in Kalwa, Mumbai. We can all learn from the way they share their love and dedication with their children, families and community, through cooking."
-Dr Darren Weiss, President, Humble Smile Foundation

Good People Fund
"Nothing makes us at The Good People Fund happier than seeing that our initial investment continues to "bear fruit" for years to come. Giving that first money for the Masala Mama's kitchen has indeed done just that! We could not be prouder of the 'Masala Mamas' and everyone else who has made GPM the success that it is today."
-Naomi Eisenberger, Executive Director, Co-Founder, Good People Fund

JDC-Grid
"JDC -GRID is a proud and longstanding partner of GPM in promoting the welfare of children, women and youth in Kalwa, Mumbai. Masala Mama's Kitchen reflects the strength and voice that mothers and grandmothers have found thanks to GPM's initiatives. The stories and recipes will nourish the soul of every reader."
-Mandie Winston, Executive Director, JDC Global Response, Innovative Development (GRID)

Sundara
"Gabriel Project Mumbai embodies the true definition of grassroots community empowerment. From the nutrition social enterprise run by the Masala Mamas, the Shravan Health Clinic, safe drinking water projects to the Joshua Greenberger Learning Center, GPM is forever assessing community needs and determining the best ways to meet them. Our team when in India can see, feel and hear the impact: jobs created, meals provided, lives saved. GPM has improved thousands of lives in an immeasurable way."
-Erin Zaikis, Founder, Sundara

The Estelle Friedman Gervis Family Foundation
"The Estelle Friedman Gervis Family Foundation is proud to support Gabriel Project Mumbai the Dr. Gerald J. Friedman Infant Malnutrition Intervention Program that it operates in the slums of Mumbai. The Foundation provides support services for children in need, including children with physical illnesses, disabilities, developmental delays or in stressful life situations. GPM is a grantee who exemplifies our mission!"
-Barbara Gervis, President, The Estelle Friedman Gervis Family Foundation

OLAM
"OLAM is delighted that Gabriel Project Mumbai is an integral part of our diverse and growing community of Jewish individuals and organizations working to engage the Jewish world in global service and international development. Through its commitment to collaboration, GPM embodies our deepest values. We are so proud of Gabriel Project Mumbai and 'Masala Mamas' and hope that the cookbook amplifies their work!"
-Dyonna Ginsburg, Executive Director, OLAM

Tzedek
"The Masala Mamas cookbook is a wonderful initiative from Gabriel Project Mumbai. Tzedek has spent the past 20 years promoting and supporting sustainable and grassroots projects that empower people, in particular women and children, to break free from poverty; and we're honoured to be one of the GPM partners in the battle to end extreme poverty worldwide."
-Dr Judith Stanton, Chief Executive, Tzedek

Sponsors

Gold Patrons
Andrew Jacobs
AGT Food & Ingredients, India

Patrons
Marshall Huebner
Tammie Slade
Marian Sofaer

Benefactors
Sari Ganulin
Valerie Gerstein
Rachel Karlin
Deborah Klein
Claire Sztokman
Isaac and Daliah Sztokman
Jack and Diane Zeller

Supporters

Ashwini Bhanushali
Dyonna Ginsberg
Jenny Hartin
Nancy Knight
Jeffrey Loewenthal

Joop Meijers
David Morrison
Molly and Philip Pollak-Gassel
Jayne Richman
Rachel Salston

Linda L Sendowski
Jane Shapiro
Lisa Silverman

Friends

Jacqueline Agami
Alissa Altman
Anna and Joel Ballin
Tina and Ralph Barnett
Ann Belinsky
Harris Berman
Nina Black
Georgina Bye
Tanya Djanogly
Sam Fleischaker
Ayala Freeman

Sari Ganulin
Peter Geffen
Andrea Grant
Sarah Gribetz
Kathe Hertzberg
Dianne Hirsh
Kandy Hutman
Elizabeth Kay
Chaim Kram
Ruth Lang
Rachelle Laytner

Joanna Maissel
Naama Margolis
Leo Muller
Rochelle Oseron
Kathy Pollard
Sarah Pritzker
Adrian Sackson
Adeena Sussman
Danielle Weintraub

index

A

aam panha, 52
agarbatt (incense stick), 34
age, 34, 100, 166
AGT Foods & Ingredients, i
Ahmednagar, 32, 84, 140
ajwain, 12, 72, 135
Alibaug, 69, 71
all-purpose flour, see maida
allergies, 25
almond pudding, 185
aloo paratha, 80
aloo samosas, 132
almonds, 185
alu wadi roll, 130
amaranth crispbread for fasting, 135
amaranth flour, see rajgira
amchur, 12, 20, 59, 131, 161, 164
anda masala, 148
anise, 13, 40, 44
anti-oxidant, 57
appam, savory, 126
appam patra, 17, 126
apples, 102, 190, 194, 199
apple bars, 199
apple kheer, 190, 194
apple pudding, 194
arranged marriages, 116-117
Arsian, Huseyin, i
asafoetida, 12
atta, 18, 23, 46, 66, 68, 72
Ayurveda, 57, 146

B

baby eggplants, stuffed, 170
badam halwa, 185, 190
baluhashi, 7, 100, 196
banana cutlets, 139
barfi, apple, 199
barfi, coconut, 191
basil seeds, see sabja
basundi, 190, 192
bay leaves, 12
bell pepper (capsicum) potato masala, 161
besan dhirde, 85
besan flour, 18, 72, 85, 92, 98, 125, 130, 137, 138
besan fritters, 118
bhaji, dill, 155
bhaji, pav, 156
bhaji, potato, 154
bhaji, upvas puri, 127
bhajji, yogurt, 122
bharli wangi, 170
bharwa bindi, 55, 131
bindis, 4, 34
biryani, 104, 140, 172
biscuits, sweet, 200
black chickpea stew, 110
black-eyed peas, 14
black gram lentils, 14

blessings, 34, 78-79
blood diseases, 52
bora berries, 100
breads, 63-76:
    classic poori, 66;
    crispbread, cumin, 67;
    crispbread, fenugreek, 68;
    crispbread, round, 66;
    crispbread, spicy, 72;
    flatbread, classic, 67;
    flatbread, spicy wheat, 72;
    methi poori, 68;
    Moshe's Jeera poori, 67;
    naan, 67;
    pav, 74;
    poori, methi, 68;
    poori, Moshe Shek's jeera, 67;
    poori, classic, 66;
    rolls, 74
    spicy crispbread, 72;
    spicy wheat flatbread, 72;
    tikhi bakri, 72;
    tikhat poori, 76
breakfast foods, 77-92:
    aloo paratha, 80;
    besan dhirde, 85;
    cheese-stuffed flatbread, 90;
    chickpea "omelet", 85;
    crepes, spicy, 82;
    dosas, rice, 81;
    flatbread, cheese-stuffed, 90;
    flatbread, potato-stuffed, 80;
    flatbread, spinach-stuffed, 92;
    fritters, tapioca, 86;
    ghavan, 82;
    kanda poha, 88;
    onion cereal, 88;
    palak paratha, 92;
    pancakes, rice-flour, 81;
    paneer paratha, 90;
    paratha, aloo, 80;
    paratha, palak, 92;
    paratha, paneer, 90;
    poha, 88;
    porridge, 83;
    potato-stuffed flatbread, 80;
    rice dosas, 81;
    riceflake cereal with onion, 88;
    rice-flour pancakes, 81;
    sabunda wada, 86;
    savory porridge, 83;
    spicy crepes, 82;
    spinach-stuffed flatbread, 92;
    tapioca fritters, 86;
    upma, 83
brinjal (baby eggplants), 170
brown lentils, 14
butter, 36

C

canning equipment, 17
capsicum-potato masala, 124, 161
cardamom lassi, 20, 40, 44, 52, 56, 82,
    105, 120, 136, 184, 185, 186,
    191, 192, 194, 195, 202
carrot pudding, 195
carrot-spinach khichdi, 146
cauliflower-potato stew, 168
cardamom, 12, 56
cashews, 38, 108
castes, 35
cauliflower, 147, 156, 168, 178
chai masala, 58
chaki belan, 16
chana dal, 14, 48. 152
chana masala, 152
chapattis, 16, 46, 84
Chavdry, Jayshree, 76, 155, 186
cheese, 42
cheese cloth, 17, 42
cheese fritters, 137
cheese-stuffed flatbread, 90
cheese stew, 108
"chef's method", 19, 40
Chefs, 69, 71
chicken, 174, 178
chickpea flour, see besan
chickpeas, 14, 85, 110, 120, 152
chickpea "omelet", 85
chickpea stew, 152
child labor, 3, 134
children, 2-3, 48, 55, 60, 84, 112
chili-mushroom pakora, 112, 114, 142
chili peppers, 13, 20, 38, 72. 80, 82,
    86, 88, 96, 108, 118, 122, 126,
    141, 142, 147, 154, 156, 158,
    167, 172, 175, 178
Chinese pulav, 178
chowli (lubia), 14
chutney:
    coconut, 101, 104;
    mango, 103;
    onion-garlic, 106;
    preparing, 17;
    tomato, 96
cinnamon, 12, 102, 147, 161, 194, 199
clarified butter, 7, 36
classic poori, 66
Clinton, Bill, 3
cloves, 12, 105, 161
coconut, 9, 20, 23, 40, 61, 88, 101,
    106, 110, 118, 122, 127, 138,
    147, 148, 162, 168, 170, 175,
    176, 180, 186, 188, 191, 195
coconut confectionary, 191
coconut dip, 101
coconut-cauliflower curry, 124, 147
coconut chutney, 101, 104
coconut-kokum drink, 61
coconut oil, 19, 95, 185
coffee grinder, 16, 19
cooling foods, 114
coriander fritters, 138
coriander (kothimbir), 12, 14, 20, 38,

40, 72. 80, 85, 86. 90, 92, 108, 114, 122, 126, 127, 131, 138, 141, 142, 146, 152, 154, 158, 162, 164, 167, 168, 170, 175, 176, 178, 180, 183
cornflour, 137
cosmetic foods, 95
crepes, spicy, 82
crispbread:
- amaranth, 135;
- crispbread, cumin, 67;
- fenugreek, 68;
- round, 66;
- spicy, 72
cucumber, 114
cumin, 12, 40, 52, 57, 59, 69, 92, 98, 110, 113, 114, 126, 131, 141, 152, 154, 155, 158, 160, 167, 168, 170, 175, 178
cumin seeds, see jeera
cumin water, 59
curd kadhi, 98, 100
curry:
- coconut-cauliflower, 147;
- "lamb", 176;
- leaves, 14;
- "seafood", 175
curry leaves, 83, 98, 101, 102, 126, 127, 131, 154, 158, 160, 162, 168, 170, 183
cutlets, banana, 139
cutlets, taro leaf, 130

D

dairy, see milk or milk products
dal (or dahl):
- dal bati, 14;
- chana dal, 14, 110, 120;
- masoor dal, 14, 183;
- moong dahl, 160, 202;
- split mung, 146, 160;
- toor dal, 14;
- urad dal, 14, 136;
- yellow mung, 155, 160
daughters, 117
Delicio women's cooperative, 2, 3, 158
deepam (light), 34
dhupam (incense), 34
diabetes, 62
diya (candle), 34
dill, 4, 155, 178
dill stew, 155
dip:
- coconut, 101;
- mango, 103;
- dip, tomato, 96;
- dip, yogurt, 114
dips, 93-114:
- black chickpea stew, 110;
- cheese stew, 108;
- chutney, coconut, 101;
- chutney, mango, 103;
- chutney, onion-garlic, 106;
- chutney, tomato, 96;
- coconut chutney, 101;
- coconut dip, 101;
- curd kadhi, 98;
- dip, coconut, 101;
- dip, mango, 103;
- dip, tomato, 96;
- dip, yogurt, 114;
- kala chana amti, 110;
- kanda lasun chutney, 106;
- mango chutney, 103;
- mango dip, 103;
- mango preserve, 105;
- mango pickle, 113;
- masala, paneer, 108;
- muramba kairicha, 105;
- onion-garlic spice mix, 106;
- paneer masala, 108;
- pickled mango, 113;
- preparing, 17;
- preserve, mango, 105;
- raita, 114;
- stew, black chickpea, 110;
- stew, yogurt, 98;
- stew, white cheese, 108;
- tomato chutney, 96;
- tomato dip, 96;
- white-cheese stew, 108;
- yogurt dip, 114;
- yogurt stew, 98
divorce, 116-117
Doctors for You, 150-151, 206
dosas, rice, 81
dough, 16, 18-19, 66, 67, 84, 90, 92, 128-129, 132-133, 135, 141, 156, 186, 188, 196
Dr. Gerald J. Friedman Infant Malnutrition Intervention Program, 150-151
dried fruit, 65, 83, 186, 188, 192
drinks, 49-62:
- aam panha, 52;
- cardamom lassi, 56;
- coconut-kokum drink, 61;
- cumin water, 59;
- faluda, 62;
- jal jeera, 59;
- kokum fruit drink, 57;
- kokum sharbat, 57;
- lassi, cardamom, 56;
- lassi, mango, 53;
- limbu sharbat, 58;
- mango lassi, 53;
- mango-yogurt drink, 53;
- milkshake, 62;
- raw mango drink, 52;
- sharbat, kokum, 57;
- sharbat, limbu, 658;
- sol kadi, 61;
- sweet lemon juice, 58;
- yogurt drink, 56
dumplings, sweet, 196
Dsouza, Hayley, 95, 110, 112, 113, 142

E

Eat2Learn, 4, 48, 134
education, 3, 48, 54-55, 104, 134, 166
egg curry, 100, 148
egg pulav (pilaf), 4, 158
egg stew, 148
eggplants, stuffed, 170
Engelmayer, Jay, 118
Estelle Friedman Gervis Family Foundation, 151, 207
Ezee Paste, 150-151

F

faluda, 62
faral, 10, 79, 180, 190
fasting, 18, 64
fasting foods, see also upwas:
- amaranth crispbread, 135;
- potato bhaji, 127;
- spongeball snacks, 141
feet-falling, 34
femicide, 145
fennel, 12, 40, 59, 113, 120, 131
fenugreek leaves, see methi
fenugreek (methi), 12, 14, 68, 128
fenugreek pastries, 128
fertility, 140
festivals, 9-10, 55, 78-79, 120;
- Diwali, 10, 190, 200;
- Ganesh Chaturhi, 78, 186;
- Gudi Padwa, 100;
- Makar Sankranti, 10, 78;
- Nag Panchami, 10, 78
fish, 9, 174, 175, 180
"fish" masala, 180
flatbread:
- sweet-stuffed, 120;
- flatbread, cheese-stuffed, 90;
- flatbread, classic, 67;
- flatbread, potato-stuffed, 80;
- flatbread, spicy wheat, 72;
- flatbread, spinach-stuffed, 92
flours, 18-19, 23, 46, 66, 67, 72, 127, 135
food security, 2-3, 134
Friedman, Dr. Gerald J., 150-151
fritters:
- coriander, 138;
- cheese, 137;
- fritters, gram flour (besan), 118;
- fritters, lentil, 136;
- fritters, onion, 125;
- fritters, tapioca, 86;
- fritters, yogurt, 122
fullower batata rassa, 168

G

Gabriel Project Mumbai (GPM), i, ii, I, 2, 6, 144-145, 158, 205-206
Gaikwad, Alka Harishchandra, 34, 52, 72, 98, 100, 118, 196
Gaikwad, Ranjana Ramchandra, 34, 66, 152, 160
gajar halwa, 4, 195
galub jamun, 140, 184
gandham (sandal paste), 34
garam masala, 7, 40, 90, 106, 128, 147, 152, 156, 162, 164, 167, 168, 180, 183
garlic, 38, 65, 76, 80, 106. 110, 118, 138, 146, 148, 154, 155, 156, 158, 167, 168, 180, 183
gastro-intestinal issues, 52, 57, 62, 114
Gawde, Kalpana, 80, 96, 110, 166, 167
Gervis, Barbara, 151

ghavan, 4, 82, 104
ghee, 7, 17, 19, 36, 72. 80, 81, 105, 120, 127, 147, 164, 184, 186, 188, 194, 196, 199, 201
ginger, 13, 38, 101, 102, 122, 127, 138, 141, 152, 154, 156, 167, 168, 178
ginger-garlic paste, 38, 85, 92, 96, 137, 164, 172, 176
girls' education, 4-5, 54-55, 124, 144-145, 166
glossary, 26-30
gluten-free, 18, 25
goda masala, 7, 14
gods, 4, 35, 78-79:
    fire god, 79;
    Gram Dev Mitkova, 35;
    Jejuri Khandoba, 35;
    Lakshmi, 4, 35;
    Loni, MaVala, 35;
    Durga, 4;
    Ganesh, 4, 78;
    Shiva, 35;
    snake god, 4 , 78
    Yamia Devi, 35
Godbole, Ragini, 53, 59, 174, 175, 176, 180
Good People Fund, 3, 207
gram flour, see besan
gram flour fritters, 118
Greenberger, Penny and Bob, 134
Gujarat, 9, 40

H

hair, 62, 95
halad (yellow powder), 34
halwa, 55:
    almond 185;
    carrot, 195
health properties of food, 8, 18, 36, 44, 52, 55, 62, 72, 95, 146
Hindi, 26-27
hing, 59, 85, 88, 92, 96, 110, 118, 131, 136, 168
hot chili hands, 20
hot meals in school, 2-5
Humble Smile Foundation, 207
hunger, 3-4, 48
Hyderabad Mix, 150-151

I

idli rack, 17
idlis, 17, 141
incense, 34
India:
    cooking, 8-11, 148;
    culture, 8, 116;
    divorce rates, 116;
    food, 8-10, 148;
    geography, 8-9;
    map, 32;
    population, 8-9
in-laws, 116-117
Integrated Child Development Program (ICDP), 150
International Year of the Pulses, i

J

Jacobs, Andrew, i
jaggery, 10, 13, 20, 52, 78, 105, 120, 138, 168, 170, 186
jal jeera, 59, 174
JDC Grid, 207
jeera (cumin seeds), 12, 50, 68, 69, 76, 85, 98, 101, 122, 127, 130, 146, 172, 176, 183
jewelry, 116
jhaara, 16
Joshua Jacob Greenberger Learning Center, 134
jowar, 18, 72, 92

K

kachori, sweet, 188
kadai (also kadhai, karahi), 15
Kadam, Kamal Shivaji, 52, 92, 103, 117, 124, 125, 128, 147, 161
Kadu, Maya, 81, 82, 101, 104, 105, 127, 172
kala chana amti, 110
Kalwa, ii; 2-6, 7-10, 84, 117, 124, 150-151, 152, 160
kanda lasun, 148
kanda lasun chutney, 106, 110, 124
kanda bhajji, 125
kanda poha, 88
kanevel, 78
Kerala, 40
kheer, apple, 194
khichdi, 48;
    carrot and spinach, 146
Khose, Subhadra, 35, 116, 136, 140, 141, 170
khoya (milk powder), 184, 188
kitchen, 7:
    essential equipment of, 15-17
    special needed, 25
kokum fruit, 9, 57, 61
kokum fruit drink, 57
Kolhapur, 162
Kondwal, Jayshree, 122, 184
Konkan Coast, 54, 174
kokum sharbat, 57
kothimbir, see coriander
kothimbir vadi, 138
kuldevi, 35
kumkum (red powder), 34

L

lafa bread, 67
lamb, 176
"lamb" curry, 176
lassi, cardamom, 56
lassi, mango, 53
leaves, 14
lemon, 58
lemonade, 58
lentil fritters, 136
lentil pudding, 202
lentil pilaf with carrots and spinach, 146
lentil stew, 160
lentils, 14, 16, 48, 96, 136, 146, 160, 202
limbu sharbat, 58

Love2Learn school, 2-3, 48, 60, 112, 134, 152, 160, 183

M

Mahamuni, Rohini, 88, 138, 168, 170
Maharashtra:
    culture, 7-10, 15;
    drinks of, 57;
    food of, 7-10, 40, 44, 62, 82, 85, 100, 101, 105, 118, 120, 128, 152, 156, 162, 164, 188, 195, 202;
    spices of, 7, 106, 108
maida, 18, 23, 46, 74, 122, 196
mains, 143-189:
    anda masala, 148;
    baby eggplants, stuffed, 170;
    bell pepper (capsicum) potato masala, 161;
    bhaji, dill, 155;
    bhaji, pav, 156;
    bhaji, potato, 154;
    bharli wangi, 170;
    biryani, 172;
    brinjal (baby eggplants), 170;
    capsicum potato masala, 161;
    carrot-spinach khichdi, 146;
    cauliflower-potato stew, 168;
    chana masala, 152;
    chickpea stew, 152;
    Chinese pulav, 178;
    coconut-cauliflower curry, 147;
    couscous, with "lamb", 176;
    curry, coconut-cauliflower, 147;
    curry, "lamb", 176;
    curry, "seafood", 175;
    dahl, moong, 160;
    dill stew, 155;
    egg curry, 148;
    egg pulav (pilaf), 158;
    egg stew, 148;
    eggplants, stuffed, 170;
    "fish" masala, 180;
    fullower batata rassa, 168;
    khichdi, carrot and spinach, 146;
    Kolhapur vegetable masala, 162;
    "lamb" curry, 176;
    lentil pilaf with carrots and spinach, 146;
    lentil stew, 160;
    masala, capsicum (bell pepper) and potato; masala, egg, 148;
    masala, chickpea, 152;
    Kohlapur vegetable, 162;
    mattar paneer, 164;
    moong dahl, 160;
    palak paneer, 167;
    paneer, with peas, 164;
    paneer, with spinach, 167;
    pav bhaji, 156;
    peas and white cheese stew, 164;
    pilaf, rice with vegetables, 172;
    pilaf, with soya chunks (TVP), 178;
    pilaf, egg, 158;
    potato, with cauliflower in stew, 168;
    potato bhaji, 154;
    potato masala, with capsicum (bell peppers), 161;

potato stew, 154;
pulav, egg, 158;
pulav, Chinese 178;
rassa, cauliflower and potato, 168;
rice, vegetable, and "chicken" pilaf; rice and lentil pilaf (khichdi), 146;
rice and vegetable pilaf, 172;
"seafood" curry, 175;
seitan "lamb" curry, 176;
shepu bhaji, 155;
soya bean (TVP) pilaf, 178;
spinach and white cheese stew, 167;
stew, chickpea, 152;
stew, dill, 155;
stew, egg, 148;
stew, lentil, 160;
stew, peas and white cheese, 164;
stew, potato, 154;
stew, served on pav buns, 156;
stew, spinach and white cheese, 167;
stew, cauliflower and potato, 161;
stuffed brinjal, 170;
stuffed baby eggplants, 170;
tofu curry, 175;
tofu masala, 180;
TVP (soya bean) pilaf, 178;
vegetable biryani, 172;
vegetable masala, 162;
white cheese with spinach, 167
malnutrition, 150-151
Mane, Indu Sona, 2-5, 35, 54-55, 56, 57, 68, 71, 83, 120, 156, 162, 172, 195
Mane, Mangal Vittal, 90, 108, 116, 126, 198, 199
mangalsutra, 116
mangoes, 9, 52, 53, 55, 105, 113;
health benefits of, 52
mango chutney, 103
mango dip, 103
mango lassi, 53, 55, 174
mango pickle, 112, 113
mango preserve, 105
mango-yogurt drink, 53
Marathi:
culture, ii;
language, 26-27
marriage; ii, 4, 54-55, 60, 84, 116-117, 144, 198
masalas, 40
masala:
capsicum (bell pepper) and potato, 161;
chickpea, 152;
egg, 148;
masala, "fish", 180;
Kohlapur vegetable, 162;
paneer, 108
masala idlis, 141
masoor dal, 14
maswadi, 100, 118
mattar paneer, 164
measurement conversion, 21-24
meat, 8-9, 106, 174, 176, 178, 180
medu wada, 26, 136, 140
Mendes, Victoria, 158
methi, 40, 108, 128
methi poori, 55, 68
methi samosas, 124, 128

methi (fenugreek), 12, 14, 68, 128
migration, ii, 2-4, 54-55, 60
milk or milk products, 42-43, 53, 56, 62, 65, 69, 98, 108, 122, 126, 128, 137, 141, 142, 158, 164, 184, 185, 188, 192, 194, 195, 196, 199, 201, 202
milkshake, 62
milky dessert balls, 184
milky pudding, 192
millet, see ragi
mint, 14, 52, 58, 59, 158
mirchi kandap, 106
modaks, steamed, 48, 78, 186, 190
moong dahl, 160
moong dahl halwa, 202
mortar and pestle, 16, 19, 20, 40
Moshe's Jeera poori, 67
motherhood, 54-55, 60, 84, 140, 166, 190, 198
Mumbai, ii, 9, ii, 60, 125, 166, 174
mung beans, 14
muramba kairicha, 104, 105
mushrooms, tempura-fried, 142
mustard seeds, 13, 40, 50, 88, 98, 101, 113, 127, 138, 146, 152, 154, 155, 160, 168, 172
mysore bhajji, 122

N

naan, 7, 67
nariyal barfi, 190, 191
net strainer, 16
nutmeg, 13, 40, 102, 120, 138, 192
nuts (almonds, peanuts, pistachios, cashews), 56, 86, 108, 170, 172, 185, 188, 191, 192, 194, 195, 196, 199, 201, 202

O

oils, 19, 40
okra ("lady fingers"), stuffed 131
Olam, 207
olive oil, 19
onions, 21, 38, 65, 80, 83, 88, 90, 96, 106, 110, 114, 118, 125, 142, 148, 154, 158, 162, 167, 172,175, 176, 178, 180, 183
onion cereal, 88
onion fritters, 125
onion-garlic spice mix, 106
ovens, 7
owha, 95

P

pakoda, paneer, 137
pakora, chili-mushroom, 142
palak paneer, 167
palak paratha, 92, 124
pancake puffs, 141
pancakes, rice-flour, 81
paneer, 16, 17, 20, 42, 128:
paneer, with peas, 164
paneer, with spinach, 167
paneer masala, 108, 198
paneer pakoda, 137
paneer paratha, 90, 198

paratha, aloo, 80
paratha, palak, 92
paratha, paneer, 90
parsley, 14, 38, 85, 148
pastes, 38
pastries, fenugreek, 128
pastries, potato and pea, 132
pav, 74
pav bhaji, 55, 156
peas, 88, 147, 156, 164, 178, 183
peas and white cheese stew, 164
peppercorns, 13
phalam (fruit), 34
pickled mango, 113
pilaf, rice with vegetables, 172;
pilaf, with soya chunks (TVP), 178
pilaf, egg, 158
Pimpre, Usha, 127, 135, 137, 139, 178
poha, 48, 88
poori:
poori, classic, 66
poori, methi, 68
poori, Moshe Shek's jeera, 67
porridge, 83
potatoes, 88, 127, 128, 135, 154, 156, 168, 172, 183
potato, with cauliflower in stew, 168
potato and pea stuffed savory pastries, 131
potato bhaji, 4, 104, 154
potato masala, with capsicum (bell peppers), 161
potato stew, 154
potato-stuffed flatbread, 80
potato topping for crispbread, 127
poverty, 3, 48, 145
prasad, prasadam, 34-35, 186
preserve, mango, 105
pressure cooker, 16
pudding:
almond, 185;
apple, 194;
carrot, 195;
lentil, 202;
milk, 192
pujah (or puja), 4, 34, 64, 78-79, 140, 186
pulav, egg, 158
pulav, Chinese 178
pulav, soya bean, 183
pulses: importance of, i
Pune, 104, 198
puran poli, 55, 100, 120
puri, rajgiria, 135
puri, upvas, 127, 135
pushpam (flowers), 34

R

ragi (millet), 18, 65, 139, 141
rajira (amaranth), 18 64-65, 135
raita, 114
raiputs, 9
Rajastan, 9
rajgira puri, 135
rassa, cauliflower and potato, 168
Rathod, Dr. Raghunat, 48
Raut, Sangita, ii, 10, 35, 56, 84, 85, 86, 106, 130, 164, 202
raw mango drink, 52

rawa, see sooji
REAP, 4
red lentils, 14
rice, 40, 146, 158. 172, 179, 183:
    basis for meals, 61;
    conversion measurements, 23;
    versus wheat, 8;
    water, 44-45, 95;
        health properties of; 44-45, 146
rice dosas, 81
rice and lentil pilaf (khichdi) 146
rice and vegetable pilaf, 146
rice-flour pancakes, 81
riceflake cereal with onion, 88
rice flour, 81, 136
rock salt, 58, 86
rolling pin (belan), 16
rolls, 74
"Rose berry" dessert balls, 184

S

Sable, Manisha, 60, 61, 144, 188
sabja (basil seeds), 62
sabudana (tapioca), 18, 65
sabudana wada, 86
safarchand barfi, 198, 199
saffron, 56, 120, 185, 202
salt, 36, 65
samosas, aloo, 131
samosas, methi, 128
Sangli, 32
saris, 7
Satara, 32, 60, 124, 166, 190
savory appam, 126, 198
savory porridge, 83
seafood curry, 175
seitan "lamb" curry, 176
semolina, see sooji
sesame seeds, 13, 96, 106, 118, 138, 176
sexual abuse, 144-145
shankarpali, 48, 190, 200
sharbat, kokum, 57; limbu, 58
sheet, 48
Shek, Chef Moshe, 69, 70-71
shepu bhaji, 140, 155
shil noda, 16, 19, 40
Shravan Health Center, 150
Shrivinas, Chef Adam, 134
skin, 57, 95
snacks and finger foods, 115-142:
    aloo samosas, 132;
    alu wadi roll, 130;
    amaranth crispbread for fasting, 135;
    appam, savory, 126;
    banana cutlets, 139;
    besan fritters, 118;
    bhaji, upvas puri, 127;
    bhajji, yogurt, 122;
    bharwa bindi, 131;
    cheese fritters, 137;
    chili-mushroom pakora, 142;
    coriander fritters, 138;
    crispbread, amaranth, 135;
    cutlets, banana, 139;
    cutlets, taro leaf, 130;
    fasting foods, spongeball snacks, 141;
    fasting foods, amaranth crispbread, 135;
    fasting foods, potato bhaji, 127;
    fenugreek pastries, 128;
    flatbread, sweet-stuffed, 120;
    fritters, gram flour (besan), 118;
    fritters, onion, 125;
    fritters, yogurt, 122;
    fritters, coriander, 138;
    fritters, cheese, 137;
    fritters, lentil, 136;
    gram flour fritters, 118;
    idlis, 141;
    kanda bhajji, 125;
    kothimbir vadi, 138;
    lentil fritters, 136;
    masala idlis, 141;
    maswadi, 118;
    medu wada, 136;
    methi samosas, 128;
    mushrooms, tempura-fried, 142;
    mysore bhajji, 122;
    okra, stuffed, 131;
    onion fritters, 125;
    pakoda, paneer, 137;
    pakora, chili-mushroom, 142;
    pancake puffs, 141;
    paneer pakoda, 137;
    pastries, fenugreek, 128;
    potato and pea stuffed savory pastries, 131;
    potato topping for crispbread, 127;
    puran poli, 120;
    puri, rajgiria, 135;
    puri, upvas, 127, 135;
    rajgiria puri, 135;
    samosas, aloo, 131;
    samosas, methi, 128;
    savory appam, 126;
    spongeball snacks for fasting, 141;
    stuffed "lady fingers", 131;
    stuffed okra, 131;
    stuffed pastries, pea and potato, 131;
    sweet stuffed flatbread, 120;
    taro leaf cutlets, 130;
    tempura-fried mushrooms, 142;
    upvas masala idli, 141;
    upvas puri bhaji, 127;
    upvas rajgiria puri, 135;
    wada, kothimbir, 138;
    white-cheese fritters, 137;
    yogurt fritters, 122;
social change, 4-6, 10, 48, 145
sol kadi, 61
Solapur, 32, 100
sooji, 18, 48, 66, 83, 85, 126
sorghum flour, see jowar
Soup and Study program, 134
soya bean (TVP) pilaf, 48, 178, 183
soya chunks (TVP), 48, 178, 183
spice mix, 40
spices, 12, 19-20, 50, 106:
    differences in approaches to, 50;
    grinding, 16, 19, 50, 106;
    making masala out of, 40;
    masala dabba, 50;
    role of in Indian culture, 50;
spiciness, 20, 25
Spielman, Gloria, 131-132
spicy crepes, 82
spicy crispbread, 72
spicy wheat flatbread, 72
spinach, 92, 124, 130, 146, 167
spinach-stuffed flatbread, 92
spinach and white cheese stew, 167
split peas, 14
split pigeon peas, 14
spongeball snacks for fasting, 141
star anise, 13
status of women in India, 144-145
steamer, bamboo or pot, 17, 118
stew:
    black chickpea, 110;
    chickpea, 152;
    dill, 155;
    egg, 148;
    lentil, 160;
    peas and white cheese, 164;
    potato, 154;
    served on pav buns, 156;
    spinach and white cheese, 167;
    cauliflower and potato, 161;
    white cheese, 108;
    yogurt, 98
stuffed brinjal (baby eggplants), 170
stuffed "lady fingers", 131
stuffed okra, 131
stuffed pastries, pea and potato, 131
sugar, 23, 24, 52, 53, 56, 57, 58. 59, 74, 83, 88, 102, 127, 184, 185, 188, 191, 192, 195, 196, 199, 201, 202
Sundara, 207
sweet kachori, 188
sweet lemon juice, 58
sweet stuffed flatbread, 120
sweets, 181-202:
    carrot pudding, 195;
    coconut confectionary, 191;
    dumplings, sweet, 196;
    gajar halwa, 195;
    galub jamun, 184;
    halwa, almond 185;
    halwa, carrot, 195;
    kachori, sweet, 188;
    kheer, apple, 194;
    lentil pudding, 202;
    milky dessert balls, 184;
    milky pudding, 192;
    modaks, steamed, 186;
    moong dahl halwa, 202;
    nariyal barfi, 191;
    pudding, almond, 185;
    pudding, apple, 194;
    pudding, carrot, 195;
    pudding, lentil, 202;
    pudding, milk, 192;
    "Rose berry" dessert balls, 184;
    safarshand barfi, 199;
    shankarpali, 200
Sztokman, Jacob, 4

T

tamarind, 13, 59, 96, 130, 170, 175
tapioca, 86
tapioca flour, see sabudana
tapioca fritters, 86

taro leaf cutlets, 130
tawa, 16, 46
tempura-fried mushrooms, 142
thalis, 8-9, 34, 61
tikhat poori, 76
tikhi bakri, 72, 100
tikkas, 4, 34
tilgul ladoo, 10, 78-79
tofu, 175, 180
tofu curry, 175
tofu masala, 180
tomatoes, 90, 96, 108, 156, 162, 164, 168, 172, 183
tomato chutney, 96
tomato dip, 96
tomatoes, 96, 108
Trachtman, Audrey Axelrod, ii
turmeric, 13, 40, 72, 76, 82, 85, 88, 90, 95, 96, 113, 120, 128, 131, 135, 137, 146, 148, 152, 154, 155, 156, 158. 160, 162, 164, 167, 175, 176, 178, 180
Tzedek, 207

U

Umbarkar, Hirabai Vilas, 116, 131, 185, 191, 192, 194, 200
United Nations, l, 150-151
upma, 83
upvas, 9, 18, 64-65, 86, 127, 135, 141:
    masala idli, 141;
    upvas puri bhaji, 127;
    upvas rajgiria puri, 135
urad dal, 14, 96

V

vegan, 25, 139
veg pulav, 48
vegetable biryani, 172
vegetable masala, 162
vegetarian cooking, 104, 139, 146, 148, 158, 174, 175, 176, 178
villages, 32, 50, 98, 100, 120, 124, 140, 166, 190, 198
vinegar, 38
vrat, 9, 64, 65, 139

W

wada, kothimbir, 138
weddings, 116-117, 140
weight, 62
wheat versus rice, 8
white cheese, 42, 122
white-cheese fritters, 137
white-cheese stew, 108
white-cheese stuffed bread, 90
white cheese with spinach, 167
whole-wheat flour, see atta
women:
    castes, 35,
    childhoods, 54, 112, 113, 120, 124, 140, 166, 190;
    children. 55;
    cooking, 10, 55, 84, 100, 104, 166, 174, 185;
    cultures, 10, 79, 95, 100, 166;
    daily lives, 2, 172;
    education, 54, 100, 124, 144-145, 166, 190;
    fertility, 140;
    friendships, 2-4, 35, 54-55, 60, 79, 104, 174, 190, 198, 200;
    gods, 35
    knowledge, 7-8, 78-79, 95, 100;
    marriage, 55, 84, 100, 104, 124, 174, 198;
    menstruation, 144-145;
    migration, 2-4, 54-55, 60, 166, 190;
    status in India 144-145;
    work, 55, 60, 185, 198
World Health Organization, 150-151

Y

yellow split peas, 14
Yield 100, 183
yogurt, see milk or milk products
yogurt dip, 114
yogurt drink, 56
yogurt fritters, 122
yogurt stew, 98

about the authors

Dr. Elana Sztokman is an award-winning author, anthropologist, and educator specializing in gender in traditional societies. Her first two books, *The Men's Section* (Hadassah Brandeis Institute 2011) and *Educating in the Diving Image* (Hadassah Brandeis Institute 2013, with Dr. Chaya Gorsetman) both won the National Jewish Book Council award. Her third book, *The War on Women in Israel* (Sourcebooks 2014) won international acclaim and was the foundation of her work as Scholar-in-Residence for National Council of Jewish Women, Australia, in 2016. She writes and speaks all around the world on issues of gender, education, religion and society, and her articles have appeared in *Slate, The Atlantic, Everyday Feminism, Lilith, Haaretz, The Jerusalem Post* and more. She holds a doctorate in education and sociology/anthropology from Hebrew University in Jerusalem, is currently engaged in Rabbinical Studies at Hebrew Union College Jewish Institute of Religion in Jerusalem. She is married to Jacob Sztokman, Founding Director of Gabriel Project Mumbai.

Hayley Dsouza is the Educational Director of Gabriel Project Mumbai. She studied arts at St Xavier College and spent many years working in the travel industry before joining the GPM team. She supervises the educational programs in Kalwa, and conducts training for the teachers. She lives in Thane with her husband, Lloyd and their daughter, Faith.

acknowledgments

The Masala Mamas team would like to offer our deepest thanks to the following people who made this cookbook happen:

Naomi Eisenberger and the Good People Fund, for being the first to support the Masala Mamas by building a proper kitchen in the slum, and for continuing to believe in GPM and this work.

UK Chief Rabbi Rabbi Ephraim and Mrs. Valerie Mirvis for never-ending support and belief in our work.

Andrew Jacobs, for believing in the Masala Mamas cookbook from the beginning, and making it happen.

Huseyin Arslan and AGT Foods & Ingredients, India, for following Andrew Jacobs' lead and sponsoring the project.

Mandie Winston and JDC-GRID and Entwine for partnership and collegiality in addressing international development and service learning.

Chef Moshe Shek for generously donating his home, his teaching kitchen, and his expertise to help train the Masala Mamas.

Chef Shrinivas and Assistant Chef Manoj of the 5-star Meluha Hotel, Mumbai, for offering special cooking lessons to the Masala Mamas.

Chef Jay Engelmayer and Annie Eisen for donating so many hours – and the use of their kitchen – to recipe-testing and photography.

Ariella Zeller for hundreds of hours of editing and proofing, and for loving attention to detail.

Adit Goschalk, Ingrid Mueller, and Avigayil Sztokman for mountains of stunning, pro-bono professional photography.

Veteran food writer Adeena Sussman for offering invaluable professional counsel.

GPM board members: Sarah Gribetz, Gladys Teitel, and Shlomi Ravid, Carmi Abramowitz, Adrian Sackson and Alan Goldman for sharing and spreading, and especially Audrey Axelrod Trachtman for interviewing the women and lovingly writing about them.

Visitors to the Masala Mamas in Kalwa who offered love and friendship, especially: Bob and Carol Minkus, Matan Minkus, Jui Kemkar, Molly Pollack and Philip Gassel, Dr. Chaim and Audrey Trachtman, Naomi and Chaim Steinberger, Penny and Bob Greenberger, and Joyce and David Nachman.

Special friends in Mumbai: Nawshir Khurody, Rca Godbole, Chaya and Rabbi Israel Koslovsky, Sharon and Sharona Gulsurkar, Elijah Jacob, Nissim Pingle, Sigalith David, Herzel Simon, and Leya Elias.

Devoted friends around the world: Aviva Rosenberg, Valerie Gerstein, Sari Ganulin, Peter Geffen, Chaim and Bara Loewenthal, Roberta and Lee Schwartz, David and Aviva Janus, Sarit and Martin Kaminer, and Meylekh Viswanath.

The cheerful and eager food tasters: Avigayil, Effie, Yonina and Meital Sztokman, Claire Sztokman, Tari Sztokman, Maia Lieberman, Meital Lieberman, Noa Meltz, Sofiya Yushkovets, Noach Harel, Richard Harel and Matan Zerem.

All the amazing friends who attended Elana and Jacob's recipe-testing party and offered so much support, and Eliana Phansapurkar for the Bollywood dancing lessons.

The kitchen team: Gloria Speilman, Sharona Galsurkar, Tressa Eaton, Eliana Zeller, Rose Pollard, Gabe Davidson, and Yonina Sztokman.

Krutika Behrawala of Mid-day for editing, proofing, and consulting.

Kalpak Raut of The Thanekars and Jui Kemkar for helping spread the word.

Art Director Shoshana Balofsky, a brilliant artist and so much more - with gratitude for the vision, the color, the dedication, the sleepless nights, and the sharing of great food, great ideas, and great friendship.

Hayley Dsouza for interviews, cultural translations, all-hour queries, and being the feet on the ground for this project.

The amazing GPM staff doing the daily work: Vishakha Kamble, David Ramrajkar, Victoria Mendez, Nikkita Worlikar, Thaiza Dias, Dennis Moses, and Rishikesh Patel, as well as the teachers and medical staff at GPM.

GPM India Director Kenneth Dsouza for so many invaluable efforts on behalf of the women, for infinite energy and wellsprings of creative ideas, and for a boundless commitment to making the world a better place.

And especially my loving partner and spouse, Jacob Sztokman, Founding Director of Gabriel Project Mumbai, whose vision of compassion for all human beings infuses everything he does and inspires everyone he meets.

Thank you, *todah, shukriya* and *dhanyavaad!*

Credits

Art Director	Shoshana Balofsky
Photography	Adit Goschalk, Ingrid Mueller, Avigayil Sztokman, Vishakha Kamble, and Bombay Arthouse
Cover	Photo by Bombay Arthouse Design by Shoshana Balofsky
Video	Bombay Arthouse
Social media	Samantha Klazkin
Recipe testing	Jay Engelmayer, Gloria Speilman and Sharona Gulsurkar
Editing and proofing	Ariella Zeller

www.masalamamas.org